24.95

T   e to

I   N G

D E   V E S

H   Safely

By Alan Northcott

WITHDRAWN

THE COMPLETE GUIDE TO INVESTING IN DERIVATIVES: HOW TO EARN HIGH RATES OF RETURN SAFELY

Copyright © 2011 Atlantic Publishing Group, Inc.
1405 SW 6th Avenue • Ocala, Florida 34471 • Phone 800-814-1132 • Fax 352-622-1875
Web site: www.atlantic-pub.com • E-mail: sales@atlantic-pub.com
SAN Number: 268-1250

Library of Congress Cataloging-in-Publication Data

Northcott, Alan, 1951-
  The complete guide to investing in derivatives : how to earn high rates of return safely / by Alan Northcott.
     p. cm.
  Includes bibliographical references and index.
  ISBN-13: 978-1-60138-295-5 (alk. paper)
  ISBN-10: 1-60138-295-2 (alk. paper)
  1. Derivative securities. 2. Options (Finance) 3. Investment analysis. I. Title.
  HG6024.A3N67 2010
  332.64'57--dc22
                              2010016800

Printed in the United States

Printed on Recycled Paper

PROJECT MANAGER: Melissa Peterson • mpeterson@atlantic-pub.com
PROOFREADER: Gretchen Pressley • phygem@gmail.com
FRONT COVER DESIGN: Meg Buchner • megadesn@mchsi.com
BACK COVER DESIGN: Jackie Miller • millerjackiej@gmail.com

We recently lost our beloved pet "Bear," who was not only our best and dearest friend but also the "Vice President of Sunshine" here at Atlantic Publishing. He did not receive a salary but worked tirelessly 24 hours a day to please his parents. Bear was a rescue dog that turned around and showered myself, my wife, Sherri, his grand-

parents Jean, Bob, and Nancy, and every person and animal he met (maybe not rabbits) with friendship and love. He made a lot of people smile every day.

We wanted you to know that a portion of the profits of this book will be donated to The Humane Society of the United States. *–Douglas & Sherri Brown*

The human-animal bond is as old as human history. We cherish our animal companions for their unconditional affection and acceptance. We feel a thrill when we glimpse wild creatures in their natural habitat or in our own backyard.

Unfortunately, the human-animal bond has at times been weakened. Humans have exploited some animal species to the point of extinction.

The Humane Society of the United States makes a difference in the lives of animals here at home and worldwide. The HSUS is dedicated to creating a world where our relationship with animals is guided by compassion. We seek a truly humane society in which animals are respected for their intrinsic value, and where the human-animal bond is strong.

Want to help animals? We have plenty of suggestions. Adopt a pet from a local shelter, join The Humane Society and be a part of our work to help companion animals and wildlife. You will be funding our educational, legislative, investigative and outreach projects in the U.S. and across the globe.

Or perhaps you'd like to make a memorial donation in honor of a pet, friend or relative? You can through our Kindred Spirits program. And if you'd like to contribute in a more structured way, our Planned Giving Office has suggestions about estate planning, annuities, and even gifts of stock that avoid capital gains taxes.

Maybe you have land that you would like to preserve as a lasting habitat for wildlife. Our Wildlife Land Trust can help you. Perhaps the land you want to share is a backyard— that's enough. Our Urban Wildlife Sanctuary Program will show you how to create a habitat for your wild neighbors.

So you see, it's easy to help animals. And The HSUS is here to help.

2100 L Street NW • Washington, DC 20037 • 202-452-1100
www.hsus.org

Dedication

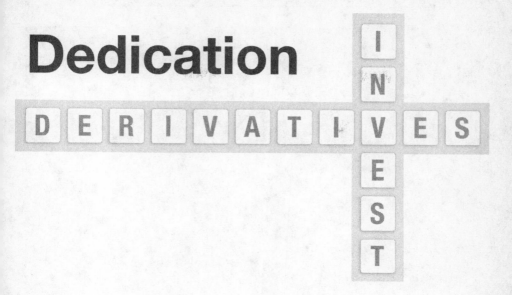

Dedicated to my beautiful wife, Liz, my constant companion through life's adventures and strength for more than thirty years.

With special thanks to Melissa Peterson at Atlantic Publishing, the editor of many of my books, and to Doug Brown, the publisher, who shares my love of and concern for animals.

Table of Contents

Introduction   13

What Does Derivative Mean?.................................... 13

Popularity.. 15

Reputation.. 16

Intended Audience... 18

Organization of Book 18

Chapter 1: Derivative Types   21

OTC vs. Exchange-Traded... 21

Forward Contracts... 24

Futures Contracts 28

Contracts for Difference 31

Spread Betting.. 32

Options 33

Swaps.. 35

Credit Contracts 37

Chapter 2: History of Derivatives   39

Origins 39

Introduction to Each Style of Derivative 41

Transference of Risks... 47

Speculation on Assets.. 48

Chapter 3: Forwards and Futures Explained   51

Equity Forwards 51

FX Forwards... 55

Forward Rate Agreement.. 57

Commodity Futures... 57

Bond Futures 66

Interest Rate Futures... 68

Equity Futures 70

FX Futures 75

Chapter 4: Contracts for Difference and Spread Betting   77

Commodities and Precious Metals CFDs 83

Equity CFDs... 86

Sector CFDs 87

Index CFDs.. 90

Currency CFDs.. 91

Chapter 5: Choosing an Option 93

American/European Styles 96

The Jargon 97

Equity Options 98

Index Options 101

Commodity Options 102

Currency Options 102

Interest Rate Options.. 104

Binary Options 105

Chapter 6: Swaps 107

Interest Rate Swaps.. 107

Equity Swap 108

Credit Default Swap.. 110

Currency Swaps 113

Chapter 7: The Underlying 115

Commodities 115

Chapter 8: The Costs 133

Pricing Forwards.. 134

Pricing Futures.. 138

Pricing CFDs 139

Pricing Options.. 141

The Greeks 151

Pricing Swaps.. 155

Trading Costs 157

Chapter 9: The Good and Bad Points   161

Versatility.. 162

Powerful 163

Hedging.. 166

Speculation 168

The Disadvantages... 170

Chapter 10: Analyzing the Markets   173

Fundamental Analysis: The Basics............................. 173

Technical Analysis – A Primer 178

Chapter 11: Constructing a Plan   199

Trading Guidelines 199

Money Management... 205

Making the Plan 207

Chapter 12: Strategies and Techniques   213

Exercising American Options 214

Covered Call 218

Naked Put... 222

Spreads 224

Hedging With Options... 226

Neither a Bear nor a Bull 232

Long Futures 235

Short Futures... 236

Chapter 13: Setting Up an Account   239

The Exchanges 239

The Brokers... 240

Opening an Account 242

Futures Contracts 243

Placing Orders 244

Chapter 14: Tax and Regulation Issues   255

Regulation 256

Conclusion   261

Glossary   265

Bibliography   281

Biography   283

Index   285

Introduction

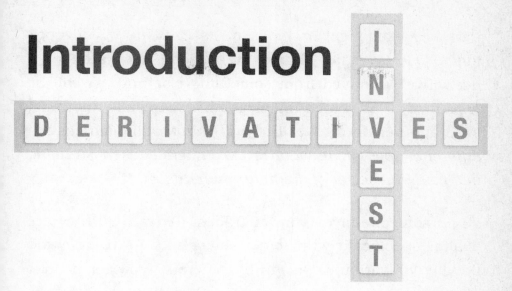

What Does Derivative Mean?

Many first encounter the word "derivative" in mathematics class, specifically when studying calculus, so for some, the word comes with some negative associations. There is no need to be concerned, as calculus does not need to figure in to the study of the different types of derivatives well known today, which are financial in nature. Although mathematical knowledge can be useful for some techniques, it is arguable that discipline and perhaps some intuition can be more necessary than any formal training in arithmetic for the trader who wants to invest successfully in derivatives.

Merriam-Webster's dictionary gives the definition of derivative as "a contract or security that derives its value from that of an underlying asset (as another security) or from the value of a rate (as of interest or currency exchange) or index of asset value (as a stock index)." It is really simple in concept; the value of a derivative is derived from something else and, as will be explained, that something else can be virtually anything, even another derivative. *The first chapter summarizes the different types of derivatives encountered when studying this powerful sector of the financial industry.*

When someone invests in, or trades, derivatives, they are dealing specifically with something created for trading and bought for various reasons by different types of people. These people may have an interest in buying or selling the underlying asset at some time for their business. For example, a manufacturer may hedge against changes in the price of raw materials, or the buyer or seller may be purely speculating on making a profit and have no other connection with the underlying asset. They are not directly buying a specific physical object but solely financial instruments that have value depending on physical or other objects, and the way the value of those objects changes. To be sure, most contracts require a specific performance at some time in the future. For instance, the contract entered into when trading a derivative may commit the holder to buy a commodity or currency at a certain price in two months time. The derivative contract itself does not convey ownership. At any time up to the performance date, the contract can be sold to a third party, and the trader will never have owned the commodity.

For example, a commodity trader may have decided in September 2009 to buy corn futures and purchased a contract for a standard quantity of 5,000 bushels of corn, for delivery in March 2010. *The term* corn futures *is explained in Chapter 3*. The price quoted was 330, which is in cents per bushel, and means the 5,000 bushels would cost $16,500 in March. Because of "margin," a way of leveraging money, the trader only needed $1,350 to get the contract and has no intention of waiting until March.

Cold and wet harvest weather hit in October, and the price rose from 330 to 410 cents per bushel. Capturing the gains, the contract was sold for a quick profit of $4,000 (410 minus 330, multiplied by 5000 bushels) — a successful trade. This realistic ability to multiply profits compared to "standard" investing — buying shares, for instance — is the reason derivatives have attracted so much attention.

Popularity

So, despite the simplicity in principle of derivatives, they are becoming increasingly popular, and for good reason. The reader of this book is assumed to have heard of derivatives and to have a natural interest in learning about them. They have many interesting features, not the least of which is multiplying the power of investment capital that can lead to large gains, far more than expected by simply depositing money in a bank or investing in stocks and shares.

In contrast to what may be considered a "passive" investment, such as a certificate of deposit (CD) or stocks and bonds, derivatives are something that requires the owner to have an active interest, and typically, investors do not expect to "buy-and-hold" derivatives for the long term. They have a time value built in and dates for certain actions are included, so the values change as time passes. As a successful derivatives investor, a trader will learn how to evaluate the effect of time and use the changes to his or advantage.

It is the possibility to attain good growth in derivatives over a short period of time, rather than needing to buy-and-hold as required by many other investments, that has really contributed to the interest in and popularity of derivatives. Derivatives, at least, give the hope rapid wealth can be attained to satisfy cravings without too much delay.

Coupled with this, the advent of the Internet has opened up many markets to the populace and made trading from home a practical reality. Now, anyone can try his or her hand at making a profit without the physical limitations that existed previously.

Reputation

Along with the advantages of rapid growth come responsibilities for wise application, and derivatives, as a class of investments, have been blamed for much of the financial crisis that hit in 2008, which shows even knowledgeable investors can make mistakes. Derivatives were a major factor in the failure of Lehman Brothers, and the insurance giant AIG was bailed out in September 2008 to sustain the markets. The particular derivative on which AIG foundered was the credit default swap, and rescuing AIG from its intended fate allowed many other financial companies, which might otherwise have sunk due to their involvement, to continue in operation.

This leads to the common view that derivatives are dangerous and may only be exploited properly by those who move in the financial circles of Wall Street and have the necessary financial acumen. This is a half-truth, as it is quite possible for anyone who does not study and pay attention to what they are doing to lose money while trading derivatives — and lose it quite quickly. There are tales of people losing their fortunes by trading "futures," a popular form of derivative, and this possibility should not be summarily dismissed but treated as a warning to take due care when beginning to trade. Many techniques can reduce the degree of risk. As with all financial trading, there are seldom guaranteed outcomes, and some losses are inevitable. The task is to play the odds in a rational manner and cut losses before they become out of hand. *Reducing risk is discussed further in Chapter 12.*

Derivatives are no longer an investment only used by those working on Wall Street — anyone can take advantage of them. Those who successfully trade in stocks and shares already know enough about the way the markets move to transfer their skills to the financially advantageous derivatives markets, and it is easy to include this capacity in any portfolio. In fact, with the financial downturn, many more people are interested in learning how to trade derivatives in order to try to make up their losses and restore their retirement accounts.

Intended Audience

The intent of this book is to demystify the world of derivatives of all types and lead the reader into an understanding that will allow them to determine where to take advantage of the benefits of this style of financial investment. The benefits can be significant. Apart from the obvious benefit of multiplying the gains of a trade if good choices are made, there are several ways in which derivatives can actually reduce the risks traders face in the normal course of investing. They can even add to regular income.

Anyone concerned about his or her financial well-being and wants to be proactive in securing his or her future should be able to benefit from the information in this book. Investors can also learn and understand current events taking place in the markets. Whether they choose to use what they have learned in their own investments will depend to some extent on the amount of time and research committed. It is certain the time spent studying the topic will be amply repaid by the benefits enjoyed.

Organization of Book

The book is designed to educate about derivatives, and it is recommended the reader initially go through it in order, as each chapter builds upon the previous information.

Once the overall concept is grasped, the items of particular interest can be returned to for a more detailed study, singling out, for instance, the chapter on "options."

Scattered throughout the book are "case studies" where experts explain experiences on various aspects of the subject. This popular format brings the, sometimes difficult to understand, ideas down to earth and shows how people are profiting right now from trading different derivatives. Several of the experts have written their own books or courses, and the contact information given allows anyone to pursue further learning on their specialist subjects. Education is a lifelong pursuit, and the traders, who are consistently profiting almost without exception, are the ones who make an effort to continue learning throughout their careers.

Chapter 1

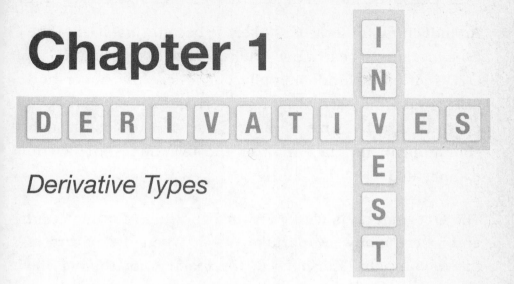

Derivative Types

This chapter provides a summary of the types of derivatives available and demonstrates the key differences of each. There are many derivative contracts that can be traded, and they generally fall into five types: forward contracts, futures, options, swaps, and credit default contracts.

There are two main ways to become involved with derivatives: in the over-the-counter (OTC) market and trading in an exchange.

OTC vs. Exchange-Traded

Whether trades are made OTC or with an exchange depends mainly on the type of derivatives being dealt in. There are some notable differences between the two types that are important to become acquainted with.

An individual trader is less likely to become involved in the OTC markets, as exchange trading is easier to execute. The OTC market is fundamentally one where the buyer and seller must find each other and work out the details of the contract directly. This is made somewhat easier through communications via e-mail or the telephone but is still complicated.

The OTC market is where forward contracts can be found and where many swaps take place. When the nature of these contracts is discussed, the reasons for this will be apparent. Despite requiring additional work to put together the deal, OTC contracts amount to many trillions of dollars each year. Information from the Bank for International Settlements shows the total value of OTC derivative contracts for the first half of 2009 amounted to more than $600 trillion, and more than two-thirds of this was in interest rate contracts. Interest rate swaps, a subsection of this group, accounted for more than half of all OTC contracts.

The advantage of OTC is each contract can be tailored exactly to suit the two parties entering into the agreement. This is important particularly for interest rate swaps, which constitute a major section of OTC dealing where standard contracts would not be suitable.

A basic difference between OTC and exchange-traded derivatives is in the guarantee of performance. With an OTC trade, there is no fundamental guarantee the contract will be honored, as the contract is just between two parties, either of which could default. For instance, a forward contract-traded OTC might be between an oil driller and a refinery and arrange for a certain number of barrels of crude oil to be delivered at a certain price on a particular day. This would be a typical way for a forward contract to be used.

If on that day, the oil driller found he could sell for much more to someone else, then he or she might not fulfill the contract. Certainly, he or she would be in trouble for doing so, as the contract could be enforced in court in due course and a claim for damages and loss of profit made. Nothing, however, forces him or her to hand over the oil or make restitution until the case has been heard and decided.

Similarly, the refiner could be in a position where the oil was accepted and no payment was made. The courts would sort out the rights and wrongs of the case in the fullness of time, but there would be no immediate solution.

Turning now to derivatives traded on an exchange, the exchange itself, as the intermediary, guarantees the contract will be performed. There is no risk associated with the transaction being completed — just the risk the trade may not end in profit. Each side of the contract will not even know who is holding the other side, and there will be no question about their creditworthiness or ability to pay.

The exchange has a couple of ways to protect itself from a defaulting client, and these include a daily "marking-to-market" and margin accounts. *These concepts will be discussed later in Chapter 3.* For now, it is enough to know "marking-to-market" means the current value of the contract is substituted each day, realizing an ongoing profit or a loss, which must be covered as it occurs. This is in contrast to the stock market, where gains or losses are only realized at the time the stock is sold. With this, the exchange client is not permitted to get to a point where losses have built up over a long period without contributing money to set against them. Trading "on margin" or with a margin account means the trader has a certain percentage of the total value of the contract already in the account.

With exchange-traded contracts, the terms are standardized so buyers and sellers know exactly what they are dealing with. The exchange itself includes "market-makers" whose job it is to act as buyers for traders wishing to sell and as sellers for traders wishing to buy. The standardization of the contracts facilitates the amount of trading taking place and provides what is called "liquidity" to the market. Liquidity means, in all normal situations, there will be buyers and sellers available and wanting to trade, which results in keen and consistent pricing.

Forward Contracts

The first type of derivative discussed here is the forward contract. This is the most basic concept, with a buyer agreeing to buy a commodity or financial asset for a certain price at a set date in the future and the seller agreeing to supply it as determined in the contract. The price is agreed in advance in the contract, so any change in the "spot," or current price of the commodity, will be reflected in how much the contract would be worth.

The forward contract has a value that "derives" from the future transaction. The essence of the speculation — or the hedge sought by entering into the contract — is both parties are happy at the time the contract is written with the agreed future price. As time passes, the price may seem to be too high or too low because of market fluctuations. This would give the speculator an opportunity to make money by selling the contract to another interested party. This other party could be another speculator hoping for a profit or someone who wants to go through with the transaction. *This will be discussed later in Chapter 3.*

If it looks as if the market price will be higher than the agreed price, the party with the right to buy at the agreed price could sell that right — his or her contract — for a profit to someone else. This individual could expect to make money on it by buying at the agreed price and selling the underlying goods immediately on the market. Similarly, the future seller might derive a profit from a lowering in price and could either wait until the due date or sell the contract for a return.

You may well have taken part in a forward contract yourself without realizing it. For instance, if you have ever bought a new car — unless the dealer was able to sell you one that fitted your requirements for color, trim level, and accessories directly from the car lot — you probably signed what is, in effect, a forward contract. The contract agreed to the price to be paid in the future and gave an expected delivery date. In this case, you fully intended to go through with the contract, accept delivery, and pay for the new car. This is not the case with all trading in forward contracts, as some may be sold on to others to make a speculative profit.

Forward contracts are customized to suit both parties to the contract and are traded OTC, which allows the contract to be agreed to individually. Forward contracts are bilateral, which means there are two parties to the contract. Despite what was previously said about parties possibly defaulting on the agreement, the forward contract should always be regarded as binding, as this is the legal status of the deal. The party in the buyer's position, which has contracted to buy the commodity or financial asset at a date in the future, is obliged to do so and cannot renege on the agreement without suffering possible legal consequences for breaking a contract. The future buyer is also referred to as the "long party," and he or she holds the "long position" on the contract. This terminology may be familiar if you have investing experience, as it is the standard way to refer to someone who has bought an asset or stock. For instance, if someone is "long on Motorola," that means he or she has bought shares in Motorola, presumably with the expectation or hope the price will increase.

The party agreeing to sell in the future is similarly obliged to sell the asset on the due date for the agreed amount. If the seller does not already own it, he or she would have to buy it at the market price in order to be able to provide it as required to comply with the forward contract, and he or she will make a profit or loss depending on whether the price is lower or higher than the contract price. As may be guessed, the seller is called the "short party," and he or she holds the "short position" on the contract. This can be compared to a stock trader going "short" on a stock, which means he or she has sold the stock and will have to buy it back later to complete the trade.

It is more likely, as a private trader, you will be trading futures contracts rather than forward contracts because of the ease of doing so and their standard nature. However, forward contracts account for a significant amount of trade, usually with at least one party being a bank or financial house. The most common forward contracts are probably in the foreign exchange (FX) market, and companies that deal internationally will use these contracts to provide stability and predictability to their international operations.

Commodity forwards are also common in the energy industry. Anyone who follows the markets will notice the price of a barrel of oil often fluctuates greatly. It is hard to run a business successfully with such variations, so typically the companies involved will smooth out the peaks and troughs by agreeing on their requirements in advance using a forward contract.

Finally, though the use of forwards provides predictability, the buyer or the seller would have done better by using the spot market, which means buying or selling at the prevailing price. If the price is above the contract price, the buyer has saved some money and the seller loses; however, if the spot price falls below the contract price, the buyer loses by having to pay more than the commodity would cost on the open market and, in this case, the seller wins. The prospect of significant gains is what attracts speculators to this type of derivative contract, but it also means a speculator can be burnt. What one gains the other loses. This outcome is typical for transactions like these.

Futures Contracts

A futures contract is a standardized form of a forward contract, which is traded on an exchange. This makes buying and selling these contracts easy, and consequently, futures contracts, or simply "futures," are popular with speculators, investors who are prepared to take a risk in return for the opportunity to make large gains. Speculation is sometimes equated with gambling, but it involves skill, experience, and insight, as well as a little luck. There are several exchanges where futures can be traded. *These exchanges will be discussed later in Chapter 13.*

A futures contract is an agreement to buy or sell a certain quantity of a commodity or financial asset on a certain date at a certain price, exactly as with a forward contract. The differences to be noted are:

- Futures are traded on an exchange, and this means each party to the contract has no idea who the other party is.

- The exchange ensures the contract is guaranteed to be executed, and it is not subject to default by either party.

- The exchange also provides liquidity, with an adequate supply of potential buyers and sellers for each contract that ensures the contract can normally be bought or sold when wanted.

- The exchange defines the quantity and quality of the commodity involved in the transaction and the delivery date, and trading futures means choosing a standard predefined contract.

- Each trading day, the contracts are "marked-to-market," which causes a financial adjustment to take place.

A term used in derivatives is the "underlying" or "underlier." This refers to whatever the futures contract or other derivative is based on — the crude oil, for instance, in the example previously mentioned. The futures contract is the commitment to buy or sell the underlying at a future date but is traded in its own right, and profits are made from its fluctuating value, which does not always fluctuate in line with the price of the underlying. Frequently, the underlying is a commodity, which is how the future market developed originally, allowing producers and manufacturers to protect their businesses against large changes in the price of goods to be delivered in the future. In the last few decades, financial underliers have become dominant, and speculation is now a major force in all derivative markets. *Chapter 7 discusses the different types of underliers that you will encounter.*

As mentioned previously, marking-to-market means the value is updated every day. A futures contract will vary in value according to how the value of the underlier changes and how the market perceives the price changing before the delivery date. For example, if there is a contract to buy something for $30 next month, and the current or spot price has already risen to $35, it is likely the contract could be sold to another trader for a few dollars profit. Pricing of a derivative can become complicated even though the fundamentals are easy to understand, and it is such an important part of trading for a profit that an entire section of this book is devoted to the subject. *Chapter 8 will discuss this more specifically.*

Bank for International Settlements information for the futures market is assembled every quarter. The latest figures show a notional futures market of nearly $20 trillion for the second quarter of 2009. Because of the way futures work, this is the principal involved and does not indicate the amount of money being used for speculation, as is clarified in the detailed discussion of futures. The vast majority of this trading is in interest rate futures, with equity and currency (FX) futures a distant second and third.

Contracts for Difference

Although not well known in the United States, contracts for difference (CFD) have become widely used by traders in other parts of the world. CFDs are derivatives that derive their value from the price difference in the underlying security or commodity between when you bought into the CFD and when you choose to exit your position. U.S. residents are likely to be unfamiliar with CFDs because they are not permitted in the United States yet, as the Securities and Exchange Commission (SEC) exercise stricter investing controls on the markets than in some other countries.

A CFD is similar to a futures contract and can be used to hedge against large movements in price. However, it is a simpler trading tool recognized as being mainly traded by speculators for profit as having no set settlement date or standard size and is always cash settled.

Like futures, CFDs are marked-to-market and are traded on margin. The leverage factor is typically ten or 20 to one, which gives traders an excellent opportunity for good returns.

CFDs are a comparatively new invention. They were created in London approximately 20 years ago and were originally based on the idea of equity swaps, which create a payment for the difference in the future value between two sources of cash flow. *Equity swaps will be covered later in Chapter 6.* They are quite often used to get around taxes and legislation when investing.

Because of the way they were set up, CFDs got around paying the UK stamp duty and were used by hedge funds and institutional investors to hedge their stock investments. In a few years, they became available for the ordinary investor and are now available in several other countries, most notably Australia, where they are rapidly progressing to the trading tool of choice.

Spread Betting

Becoming eclipsed by CFDs to a certain extent, spread betting is comparable in many ways and can be traded similarly. Another financial tool popular in the UK because betting attracts no taxes, it is leveraged in the same way as CFDs and involves taking a calculated view of whether a stock or index is going up or down. The spread is the difference between the bid and ask prices, and there is no separate dealing fee or commission charged by the bookmaker, which means spread betting is easy to understand.

The spread better will typically "bet" a certain amount, say £1, per point of movement in the underlying. For example, say you were quoted a bid price of £100 for ZZZ Moving and an ask price of £103. If you thought the share price was going to rise, you could bet £2 for every £1 it goes above £103. If it goes up to £120, you would receive £17 (120 minus 103), but if it fell to £95, you would have to pay £8 (103 minus 95). If you wanted to bet the other way, on a declining price, your base price would be £100. Now, if it went down to £95, you would receive £5 (100 minus 95), but if it went up to £120 you would have to pay £20 (120 minus 100).

Spread betting is a cheap way of becoming involved in the price of shares or indexes and has the advantages and disadvantages of derivatives in multiplying the effects of your money. Usually, the spreads are a little larger than with CFDs, and spread betting is a little less flexible, with expiration dates similar to futures contracts.

Options

Another way to approach trading derivatives is to consider options. Options are contracts for a future transaction, as with forwards or futures, but the buyer is not required to go through with the transaction. If the buyer finds he or she has made a bad choice and will not profit from the transaction agreed, he or she can just ignore it and let the delivery date pass without having to buy or sell anything.

This prevents the buyer from having to take a loss, which must be done when trading futures if the market runs in the wrong direction. If the trader has made a profitable choice, he or she will make gains. If not, the trader does not have to suffer the potential losses of the pick.

The downside to this way of trading — and, of course, there is one — is to get an option contract, it must be paid for. The amount spent to get an option contract is called a "premium." If the option makes money, that offsets the premium already paid. If the option goes the wrong way and it will not make a profit from taking up the transaction, the buyer still loses the premium paid, even though the additional losses a futures contract would entail are avoided.

Regardless, many traders find they are more comfortable trading in options than futures. The crux of the matter is an option limits the risk. All that can be lost is the premium, and the trader is not obliged to go through with a transaction that would cost more money.

If an option will make a profit, based on the current pricing of the underlying, it is said to be "in the money." The opposite of this, when it would not be worth taking up the option, is called "out of the money." An option where the contract price is exactly the same as the spot price is called "at the money." When an option is in the money and the trader takes the profit, he or she is said to "exercise the option." The option "derives" its value from the underlying and is a popular form of derivative. When it is "out of the money" by a long way, it has little value and can be bought cheaply, as there is only a remote chance of making a profit, but changes in the price of the underlying may make it profitable.

There is other jargon associated with the world of option trading, such as "puts" and "calls," and it is possible to take the other side of an option and receive a premium for an agreement to satisfy the option if needed. In this case, as a "writer" of the option, the position taken on is not discretionary. If the option ends up in the money, the writer is obliged to satisfy the contract. *These and other factors relating to options will be discussed in Chapter 5.*

Swaps

Swaps are an interesting financial tool. A swap is an agreement or contract to exchange cash flows happening in the future. These could be based on many different underliers, but often the underlier is money. The price of money over time is interest, and the cash flows arise from interest payments.

Some may wonder why anyone would desire to exchange or swap interest rates. The rates are either the same, in which case there is no reason to make any swaps, or they are not the same and the party who would be paying more is unlikely to agree to the swap. The key to understanding their utility is to realize most interest rate swaps involve exchanging a cash flow based on a fixed interest rate with a cash flow based on a variable interest rate.

For instance, a business may borrow from a commercial bank and take out a loan where repayments are based on a variable interest rate pegged to a published rate such as the London Interbank Offered Rate (LIBOR). This is a standard interest rate published in *The Wall Street Journal* banks use when lending to each other. Typically, the loan to the business would be at a rate of LIBOR plus a fixed number of percentage points, or margin.

The owners of the business may want to have more certainty when making future cash flow projections, so they would like to have a fixed rate. They could seek to do an interest rate swap, which would be an OTC transaction, and agree to a fixed rate for the life of the loan. There are financial institutions specializing in swaps, and by a process of negotiation, they would reach agreement on the fixed rate paid in exchange for the institution taking over responsibility for paying the floating rate.

The notional amount of the swap would be the principal on which interest was due; this amount of money is not directly involved in the actual transaction taking place. The only payments contracted to be paid are the interest installments.

This is the most basic of swaps, and many complications may be brought into the transaction. Sometimes, swaps are between two different standards of interest rate, for instance LIBOR and prime rate, and sometimes, the swaps are between different currencies where fluctuating exchange rates will affect the cost to each party.

Interest rate swaps are different from the previous types of derivatives considered, as they are based on two underlying factors, the two interest rates, so the value of them varies because of the relative differences between the rates and not because of the current price of one underlier.

Credit Contracts

The final type of derivative to be discussed is the credit contract, and this has a fundamental difference from the previous ones. All the others have risk associated with the price of the underlying, and to make a profit, the trader must correctly anticipate the price movements. Credit derivatives, on the other hand, have a risk associated with whether another party will fulfill their financial obligations.

"Credit default swaps" (CDS) were the reason American International Group (AIG), the largest U.S. insurance underwriter, had to receive government financial support in September 2008 in order to keep operating. The economic downturn in 2008 dramatically affected the viability of AIG Financial Products Corp., an associated business that had been trading CDSs for ten years.

CDSs are essentially insurance policies against borrowers defaulting on their obligations and are a recent invention that, initially, appeared to be a good idea. For consumer safety, regulations require banks hold a certain amount of cash in reserve to cover any risk of some customers failing to pay. It is rumored employees of J. P. Morgan thought up the concept of the CDS in 1994 as a means of allowing banks to lend more freely. The CDS allows banks to make regular payments to a third party, and in return, the third party would guarantee payment of particular loans on their books. This would allow the bank to disregard the risk of default on those loans and not need such large reserves. Alternatively, the bank could lend more with the same cash reserves, which allows the bank to increase its business and potentially make more profit.

The insurance only covers specific risks. For instance, if a bunch of mortgages were included in a CDS, the payment may only happen if the mortgages were defaulted on. If the underlying properties lost value, there would be no compensation.

Credit derivatives are usually traded OTC, and there are other types beyond the CDS, but CDSs have achieved the most notoriety. All credit derivatives cover the risk of default caused by specific "credit events," such as bankruptcy, and are not concerned with specifics such as the rates of interest and prices.

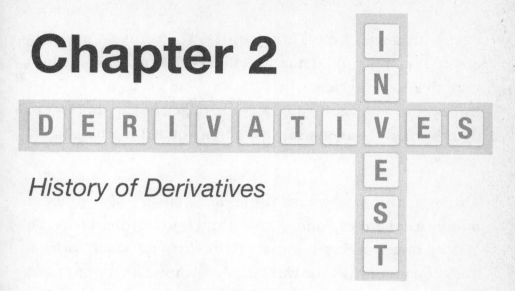

Chapter 2

History of Derivatives

Origins

For a topic that has so recently come to the fore, the origin of derivatives can be traced back many centuries, and some say even to pre-Christian times. Although there is an argument saying the ancient Greeks were familiar with the idea of options, history can certainly validate the medieval practice of European sellers agreeing and signing contracts for delivery of goods at a later date was a means of creating forward contracts. Rice traders in Osaka even produced a type of futures contract with standardized amounts in the 17th century by creating vouchers for rice purchased "on margin" for a small deposit and freely traded between participants.

Perhaps the most famous story from that period involving speculation in futures is that of the Dutch tulip mania. Tulips were unlike any previously known flower when they were introduced from Turkey in the 16th century, and this created interest and demand. Tulips are slow to bloom and take five to ten years when grown from seed and at least three years when cultivated from an offset, so the shortage of plants when the demand was increasing led to inflationary pressures.

Although the first years of the 17th century saw interest mainly from professional growers and horticulturists, by the 1630s, many others had noticed the rapidly rising prices, and the common person was tempted to invest in the prospect of high returns. Many people began trading in the bulbs because they believed prices would continue to rise, and some sold or mortgaged their homes in order to invest in the craze. It became acceptable to buy in the winter for delivery in the summer, as the offsets could only be delivered when the bulb was lifted, and by 1636, there was a thriving futures market.

Speculation escalated, with some buyers not even having the cash for their commitment and some sellers not even owning the bulbs, each convinced ever-increasing prices would continue and they could time their trading in order to profit. In February 1637, common sense prevailed, and the whole market collapsed. It took many months for the affair to unwind, with the burgemeesters, or mayors, decreeing the defaulting buyers would pay a 3 ½-percent fee as compensation to the sellers who kept their bulbs. This was not satisfactory to either party.

Introduction to Each Style of Derivative

As the markets developed, the role of derivatives was more clearly defined. In Amsterdam in the 17th century, the stock exchange developed a system of option trading, where agreements were made to buy or sell shares at a time in the future for a pre-agreed price. This was the true forerunner of the modern day trading systems.

In the New World, the New York Stock Exchange (NYSE) was founded in 1792 and almost immediately allowed trading in stock options. However, in the next century, when London became acknowledged as the center of trade for the European markets, derivatives were commenced in the London Stock Exchange. Still controversial, there was some opposition in the 1820s, with traders arguing against the principle of options and others seeing the increase in trading associated with options as a good thing because they added liquidity to the markets. The ruling committee of the London Stock Exchange even suggested banning the availability of options but was forced to relent when it became apparent a number of the members would not stop short of founding a competing stock exchange if this was done.

A major step toward the markets as we know them today was taken in 1848, when the Chicago Board of Trade (CBOT) was founded by a number of merchants. The location was key, as the railroad had opened up the trading routes, and Chicago was starting to emerge as a center for transportation between the Midwest producers and the flourishing and populous East Coast of the United States.

Initially, the contracts were forward contracts, individually negotiated and between two parties. The first such recorded contract was for corn and was traded in 1851. The use of such contracts rapidly grew but was not without troubles, mainly from nonperformance or defaulting on the contracts. This led to the CBOT standardizing the futures contract for grain in 1865 and demanding collateral from the participants to encourage performance. This collateral is now called the "margin requirement," and in those days, it was better thought of as a performance bond.

Although the origin of such derivatives was for good trading and business reasons, as with the Dutch tulip mania, it became clear gambling or speculation on future values could be lucrative for those who anticipated the price moves correctly. The growth in interest from speculators really started with the advent of standard futures contracts with assured performance. This made dealing with buying and selling grain more of a financial rather than agricultural prospect. Unlike the previous market participants, who were typically food producers and food processors, the speculators did not need to know much about the products and could simply review market trends and make their trades. The liquid market allowed them to make their deals and sell on the contracts for a profit before the delivery dates, which meant they did not need to concern themselves with the physical delivery of the commodity.

Following the success and interest in trading these markets, a number of other exchanges sprang up around the United States. New York remained centered on stock trading rather than futures, but the New York Cotton Exchange was formed in 1870. In Chicago, still the main are for futures trading, the Chicago Butter and Egg Board was founded in 1898, which evolved into the Chicago Merchant Exchange (CME), still a major force, in 1919. Exchanges were also formed in Milwaukee, St. Louis, Minneapolis, New Orleans, Memphis, Kansas City, and San Francisco.

Although futures contracts were developed for a wide range of physical underliers in the first half of the 20th century, it was not until the 1970s that futures contracts were developed, which were not based on a physical commodity. Many references call out the introduction of futures contracts on seven foreign currencies by the CME in 1972 as the first financial-based futures, and this is nearly correct. As CME themselves report, there was an attempt to introduce futures contracts on currencies in 1970. This effort was made by the New York Produce Exchange, which renamed itself the International Commerce Exchange (ICE). Leo Melamed, Chair of the CME Group, describes this as "more or less a glorified currency exchange in foreign currency geared for small-time gamblers," and says this was a far cry from the global FX futures market CME created.

The effort in 1970 was somewhat premature, as the Bretton Woods Agreement was established in 1945 and fixing exchange rates was still in force. Melamed says it took a feasibility study written by the venerable Professor Milton Friedman in 1971 to establish credibility for the idea of FX futures. In it, Professor Friedman wrote, "It is highly desirable that this demand be met by as broad, as deep, as resilient a futures market in foreign currencies as possible in order to facilitate foreign trade and invest-ment." The Bretton Woods Agreement collapsed as a result of President Nixon withdrawing the right to have dollars redeemed in physical gold, which abolished the "gold win-dow" unilaterally on August 15, 1971. Eight days later, all major currencies (except the yen, which took five addition-al days) abandoned fixed exchange rates and allowed their currencies to "float," or vary in relationship to each other.

In 1973, the Chicago Board Options Exchange (CBOE) was founded initially as an offshoot of the CBOT. This was an important step in making the options market more accessible. Prior to the CBOE, stock options were OTC and traded informally. The CBOE standardized the available option contracts and gave the guarantee of performance an exchange can provide. The interest in options increased, and other exchanges produced their own versions. In 1983, the CBOE introduced the concept of options on stock market indices, such as the Standard & Poor's 500 (S&P 500).

In 1976, the CME started issuing futures contracts on U.S. Treasury bills and, in 1982, extended its range to include exchange-traded options on bond futures. An option is a derivative with its value dependent on the underlying, in this case bond futures, and futures are similarly derivatives, so this is an example of a derivative of a derivative. It is thought in 1982 the first interest rate swap was agreed, and such OTC trading has exploded. Use of derivatives has escalated as traders and financial institutions look for more "efficient" ways to use their investment capital.

CASE STUDY: A MARKET
MAKER'S EXPERIENCE

Dan Passarelli
Author of Trading Option Greeks
and founder of Market Taker
Mentoring LLC™
www.markettaker.com
dan@markettaker.com
twitter.com/Dan_Passarelli

*Dan Passarelli is the author of the book Trading Option Greeks and founder of Market Taker Mentoring LLCTM. Market Taker Mentoring provides personalized one-on-one mentoring for option traders. The company website is **www.markettaker.com**.*

Passarelli started his trading career on the floor of the Chicago Board Options Exchange (CBOE) as an equity options market maker. He also traded agricultural options and futures on the floor of the Chicago Board of Trade (CBOT). In 2005, Passarelli joined CBOE's Options Institute and began teaching basic and advanced trading concepts to retail traders, brokers, institutional traders, financial planners and advisors, money managers, and market makers. In addition to his work with the CBOE, he taught options strategies at the Options Industry Council (OIC).

*Dan can be reached at dan@markettaker.com. He can be followed on Twitter at **www.twitter.com/Dan_Passarelli**.*

I trade options mainly. I prefer options because they have much more versatility than 'linear trading' instruments. In addition to direction, traders can exploit volatility, time, and interest discrepancies.

The thing that led me to trading in derivatives was, to some extent, geography. Chicago is my hometown and, arguably, the center of the universe for derivatives. That being said, I have always had an interest in trading, even as a small child. As soon as I learned what a stock was, I was fascinated with the whole idea of trading. Right after college, I headed straight down to the floor of the Chicago Board of Trade.

Regarding the current financial situation, the "normal" market environment is a fallacy. The market is a series of anomalies. The most recent downturn in the market was unexpected by many — or at least to the extent of the magnitude of the move. But, if a trader didn't already know to protect himself or herself from highly unlikely and unexpected moves, he or she knows now. I have lived through many highly improbable moves in my days as a market maker. The market meltdown of 2008 and 2009 was yet another dramatic move in the life of the market. We have seen them before; we will see them again.

What excites me most about derivatives is the mental stimulation. The multifaceted nature of derivatives makes them a fascinating endeavor. I have loved being a trader, a student, and a teacher of derivatives. What I dislike most about derivatives is the fact their use is often criticized by people who do not fully understand their economic importance.

I think the personal qualities that help me most in my chosen career include being an aggressive, assertive individual. Certainly, that helped me in my trading-floor career. But, I also think being, sometimes, a little "paranoid" that things can go wrong has helped me as well. In trading, especially derivatives, you have to expect the unexpected.

My biggest success in derivatives? Certainly, as a market maker, I have had some trading days that by most people's standards would be considered big winning days, but I have had my share of fairly big losing days as well. Now I would say my biggest success, or rather feeling of satisfaction, is in knowing I am helping others become better traders. I really enjoy teaching traders.

Regarding challenges, trading is a constant battle, but that is what makes trading so rewarding. When you wake up in the morning, you never know what to expect. And when things go wrong, they can go really wrong. Learning to deal with adverse conditions is a challenge, but it is what, in the end, makes you a better trader.

I would advise anyone who wanted to follow in my footsteps to commit themselves to learning, immerse themselves in it, and never stop. Some of the most enjoyable moments of my career were spent as a clerk on the trading floor. There, I began my education in options. I spent hours on the trading floor learning the intricacies of the Greeks and other nuances of options. Then, after the close, I would hang out in the office tinkering with simulated trades and studying the actual trades that traders made that day. This is when my love affair with derivatives began. And, to be successful in this business, you have to love it.

Transference of Risks

One of the major advantages with derivatives is the transference of risk. If used correctly, derivatives will reduce the individual or institution's exposure to risks that may not be acceptable, and they allow the finances to be managed efficiently. This is one factor that led to such contracts being devised in the first place.

The farmer who wishes to ensure return on a crop will be sufficient to cover expenses and create a reasonable profit can use forwards or futures to lock in the future price. The risk the price will fall and not cover the costs and overheads can be eliminated. The risk is assumed by the other party, who may see the prospect of a healthy return worth taking on the gamble.

As mentioned in the "Credit Contracts" section at the end of Chapter 1, a bank with many loans on its books can use a derivative — a credit default contract — to protect itself against the consequences of several parties defaulting. This enables the bank to continue its operations more smoothly and with less risk. The other party takes on the risk, usually for receipt of a regular premium from the bank and takes the view the risk can equate to reward.

Speculation on Assets

The other side of the risk coin is speculation, which some people equate to gambling, where the trade is made for the prospect of high returns. The majority of derivative trading taking place today is for the profit potential rather than to hedge against risk. However, speculation is not as random as gambling, but rather an assessment of the risk and reward and the chances of each outcome. Despite what some people may tell you, trading involves taking losses as well as making gains, and the successful trader manages to make the profits outweigh the losses.

Speculation for large returns has become the focus of the derivative markets because the money invested is leveraged and can achieve higher gains than simple investing. In recent years, hedge funds have become popular because they are unregulated in what they can invest in, and they tend to use leveraged products to compete with other funds on the size of return. Many financial institutions have adopted the same style of investing in order to make more money for the principal's bonuses and shareholder dividends, and sometimes, the judgments are not proved sound.

In 1995, Nick Leeson of Barings Bank became involved in making speculative trades in Japanese futures, and this was the downfall of that institution. Barings Bank was the oldest merchant bank in Great Britain, and Leeson operated out of the Singapore office, where it seems he was given free rein because of his background and previous success in the firm. The story is he was trading with an unused account number and covering his losses, which were consistent for a while, by falsifying accounts.

There have been several more tales of derivatives leading to the bankruptcy of companies, with many taking place in recent history. Bailouts of "too big to fail" (TBTF) companies, such as J. P. Morgan Chase, Bank of America, and Wells Fargo, in the financial crisis of 2008 and 2009 have become increasingly unpopular, and many of these companies have been caught by the economic situation exposing bad risk control and management when trading in exotic financial instruments, such as complex derivatives.

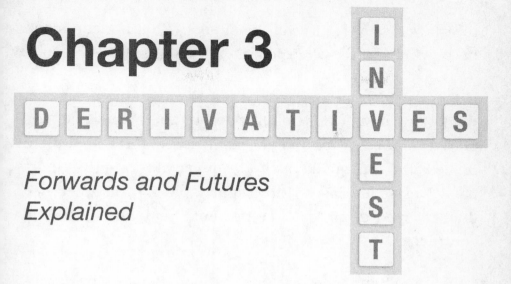

Chapter 3

DERIVATIVES

*Forwards and Futures
Explained*

F orwards and futures are similar in concept. The chief
difference is futures are easier to trade, as they can
be bought and sold on an exchange. They each involve a
contractual commitment to buy or sell the underlying at a
future time at a set price. Forwards, discussed first in this
chapter, are individual and unique contracts, and futures
are standardized contracts.

Equity Forwards

The forward contract is between two parties and specifies
a particular date, company, number of shares, and price.
On the day named, the "delivery day," one party sells the
shares as specified to the other party at the agreed price.
Before the day, it may be difficult to determine who will
win and who will lose on the transaction. It will depend on

the market or spot price of the shares. What is clear is one party wins and the other loses.

If the agreed price is greater than the current spot price, the "long party," who is obliged to buy the shares, will pay more than necessary and effectively loses. If the spot price exceeds the contracted price, the buyer wins and the "short party," or seller, loses. Either party paying the difference due, referred to as "cash settlement," may also settle the contract.

Other familiar terms include a "long forward position," which is what the trader who agrees to buy the shares in the future has taken up, and a "short forward position," which applies to the trader who agreed to a forward sale of the shares.

Forwards are OTC contracts that usually include a bank or financial institution on one side. They are frequently used by such companies to structure financial deals to meet their needs.

The mechanics of a forward contract should now be clear, but perhaps some are wondering how they are figured out in practice. As they are individually tailored to the contracting parties' requirements, there is no standard way for them to be traded, but the markets have developed many standard forms of contract to include the necessary clauses. This can be used and modified as required and will cover all the basics without needing to be renegotiated each time.

When two parties enter into a forward or a futures contract, they may have different motives. Some parties will be hedging their position and reducing risk in some way, and other parties seek to speculate in the hope of making a profit. The hedgers may be prepared for the contract to cost them a certain amount if prices change as expected before the delivery date, as this represents the cost of the "insurance" the contract provides against whatever risk is being hedged against. The speculator will be hoping for prices to move dramatically in his or her direction.

In the case of equity forwards, the short party could buy the shares at the same time as the execution of the contract and hold them until the delivery date. This idea sets a limit on what price will be put on the contract. If the contract price was sufficiently high, the short party would be sure to gain from this strategy and thus would borrow money and pay some interest in order to buy the shares straightaway.

Thinking like this helps the two parties determine what would be a fair price for the delivery in the future. The process applied to such considerations is called "cash-and-carry," a standard way in which the price of many derivatives may be calculated. The idea is in a perfect market, there should not be "arbitrage" opportunities, or if they exist, the market will act efficiently and quickly to eliminate them. Arbitrage means money can be made risk-free by taking advantage of discrepancies between different marketplaces. Arbitrage may take place with the price of physical goods or may be applied to the financial and derivative market.

The "cash-and-carry" method assumes the short party does indeed buy the shares now and holds on to them until the delivery date. "Cash" now buys the shares, and the cost is "carried" until the completion of the transaction. The rate of interest at which the cash can be borrowed is assumed, and the fair price is derived from the total cost. In the case of shares, which may have dividends, these too are factored into the calculation to determine an exact value. *These methods of valuation and variations are covered in greater depth in Chapter 8.*

For now, it is sufficient to note the theoretical position of absolute balance defined above may not always exist. There may be slight differences from the calculations that do not resolve themselves. This is because there are always other costs associated with transactions, and these may make realizing the arbitrage not cost effective. There will usually be transaction costs and brokerage fees that whittle away at the profit and may make the arbitrage unprofitable. Interest rates can also vary, so the strictly notional derivation of the derivative value may not be adhered to.

As a simple example, without considering commissions or dividends, say you wanted to have a forward contract to buy 100 shares in IBM in six months time. IBM is currently trading at $130. If you assume a no-risk interest rate of 4 percent per year, the $13,000 needed to buy the shares now would cost about $260 in interest over the six months, depending how often the interest was compounded, that is, interest added on interest. Keeping it simple, the fair market delivery cost for this contract is $13,260, or $132.60 per share.

FX Forwards

When dealing with international transactions, there is good reason for a business to enter a forward contract. Such a contract locks in the exchange rate and manages the currency risk. Certainly, a forward contract effectively surrenders any possibility of an adventitious gain from currency exchange rates moving in a favorable direction, but many companies would far sooner guarantee the rate they will receive and control their spending.

In an ordinary foreign exchange transaction, when foreign currencies are bought and sold, or exchanged, on the forex, or FX, market, it is called a "spot" deal. A typical spot FX deal is an agreement to exchange currencies at a certain rate in two business days' time, which allows time for the process to take place. This is the usual timing and is not considered a "forward contract." The day when the currencies are actually traded is called the "value date." In the terms of the FX market, this transaction takes place "for value spot." The exception to this timing is when U.S. and Canadian dollars are exchanged, which only take one business day to resolve. Thus, an FX forward is defined as any contract to swap currencies at an agreed date later than the usual value date for spot trades.

As with all forwards, the contract is binding and specifies the amount of each currency to be exchanged, which fixes the exchange rate. No matter what happens to the countries' currencies in the meantime, and whether it is a week or a year in the future, the currencies will be exchanged on the agreed future value date.

These contracts are valued in what is essentially a cash-and-carry way. The relative interest rates in the two currencies set the cost of carry, and together with the current exchange rate, the value can be calculated. Depending on the interest rates, the price may be less or more than the spot rate, so you might be paying less at the delivery date than it would cost you to buy the currency in advance at today's spot price.

Once again, a theoretical perfect value for the FX forward may not be exactly the price agreed. This is for a couple of reasons. There are transaction costs in exchanging currency, usually charged by having a "bid" and an "ask" price. For instance, it may cost $1.55 to buy one UK pound, but you may only receive $1.50 for each pound sterling when you buy dollars. Brokers buy at the bid price and sell at the ask price, so if you are buying sterling, the ask price the broker is prepared to sell at is $1.55. The cash-and-carry calculation also assumes the relative interest rates are not expected to change and does not account for the difference between the cost of borrowing money and the amount you would receive on investing in the currency.

Forward Rate Agreement

The forward rate agreement (FRA) is a derivative to secure a fixed rate of interest for a notional principal. Corporate borrowers who want to fix the interest rate to guard against increasing costs would use this, and then they would refer it to a benchmark rate such as the LIBOR. If the LIBOR increases, the FRA would ensure the company would not have to pay more interest on the loan.

The notional principal is not part of the transaction but is only used to determine the interest due on that amount. The company will take out a loan at a commercial bank and sign an FRA contract with an FRA dealer. If the interest the company pays to the bank for the loan is at a lower rate than contracted in the FRA, the company must pay the extra to the FRA dealer. If the interest rate increases to above the FRA rate, the FRA dealer compensates the company for the difference. The FRA effectively makes a fixed-rate loan.

The FRA is traded OTC but otherwise is similar to the interest rate futures contract. The seller of the contract might be a money manager concerned that interest rates are going to fall. If they do, he or she would be compensated by the buyer, who is paying lower interest and must hand over the extra he or she did not pay on the loan interest.

Commodity Futures

Discussion now turns to futures contracts, the more likely trading vehicle for the derivatives investor or speculator due to their liquid market and ready availability. Although not all futures are fully liquid, which means they do not have a ready market, the majority can be traded easily.

The standardization of futures contracts means they are settled on the same date, and many traders in futures use cash settlement, as they typically have no requirement for the physical product. A futures contract is a commitment to purchase the underlying for a predetermined price on the delivery date. Futures are traded at the commodities exchange and may change hands many times before the delivery date. It is estimated fewer than 4 percent of all futures contracts actually result in delivery. In view of the amount of trading, this is reassuring because there are not enough physical goods to satisfy all the outstanding futures contracts.

Unlike forwards, the trader typically does not know the other party to the contract, and the market makers at the exchange are responsible for matching up the various contracts to traders. The exchange provides a guarantee of performance, which means there is no question of either party defaulting on the contract affecting the other, a possibility with forward contracts.

In order to start buying and selling futures, the trader must provide a deposit, known as a margin, which provides some collateral to the exchange against the possibility the trader may not meet contractual obligations. The amount of deposit will vary with the type of futures being traded and is related to the maximum fluctuation expected in the price each day. Typically, it may be about 10 percent. This is different from the way margins are used when dealing in the stock market, where the level is set at 50 percent by the Federal Reserve; therefore, you must put up at least half of the cost of the shares you are trading. This is because the margin accomplishes a different purpose in futures trading. For shares, you are buying half and borrowing the other half as debt. With futures, the margin is just to cover the daily fluctuations in price.

The other major difference between futures and forwards is the mark-to-market, or the updating of the price each day. However much the value of the holding has changed, it is reflected in the margin account. If the futures have fallen in value, the amount is subtracted from the account. Depending on the policy of the exchange, this can result in the exchange or clearinghouse sending out a "margin call," a call to the trader to put more money in the account to maintain the required levels. This ensures security for the exchange against a catastrophic default situation, as losses are paid for as they are sustained.

Ignore a margin call at your peril, as the broker or clearinghouse is entitled to look after its interests and the interests of other traders by selling any securities it holds in your name to cover the call. They do not even need to consider the order in which they are sold or take any other action to mitigate any consequential losses.

Marking-to-market also carries the advantage that the margin account can grow as the value of the contracts increases, which means unlike trading in shares, the trader does not need to sell his or her holding before making a profit. The increased value in the margin account can be used to take out other contracts, but if used in this way, there is a greater possibility of a margin call later.

As futures have a time element, with a delivery date when the purchase is due to be executed, they cannot be left to accumulate value for years like stocks and shares. They are more suited for the active trader concerned with exercising money management and controlling the returns. Thus it is important to have a plan for what to do with the futures contract as time passes and the delivery date nears.

There are two principle choices. Firstly, the holder could let the futures contract run its course by paying for and arranging delivery of the underlying. A standard futures contract in pork bellies (actual slabs of bacon), one of the well-known commodities traded on the futures market, includes 40,000 pounds of "green, square-cut, clear, seedless bellies with 75 or fewer minor defects" delivered in Chicago in February, March, May, July, or August. For most people, taking delivery of this would not be a good solution, as they have no need for 20 tons of bacon, so the second alternative is to sell the contract, whether for a gain or a loss, before the due date or arrange settlement in cash. To continue trading in the commodity selected, the money from this can be rolled over into another contract that has a later delivery date.

Futures can be very volatile, so to maintain order in the trading, the exchanges impose a limit on how much a price for a contract can change in the trading day. The trading can continue, but the price cannot vary more than a prescribed amount despite market pressure. Sometimes, as in February 2008 with wheat futures, the market can repeatedly close "limit up," indicating an underlying problem with the level of pricing. This crisis was precipitated by a large cut in supply originating from crop failures. So, to enable the full process of "price discovery," by which a fair price is found from the marketplace, the regulators on the exchanges can temporarily increase the limit values, but this is not typical, and usually, the limits work as intended and prevent excessive volatility.

There are several different sectors of the commodity market in which you can specialize according to your experience and interest. No one sector is intrinsically better than another in the long term, but the suitability for futures trading varies in cycles between them. For instance, the energy futures may be better for profitable trading one year and the agricultural futures in another. Perhaps more importantly, before trading in any sector, the market should be researched and studied to make sure the causes of price movement are understood enough to be able to guess intelligently which trades to make. No matter how good a market sector may be for another person, unless you know something about the commodities and what moves their prices, you are unlikely to succeed.

One popular commodity sector is energy, as there has been so much interest in the topic in recent years. The energy sector includes oil, electricity, coal, natural gas, and similar products. There is a natural cycle with these commodities, based on the time of year. For example, more heating oil is sold in the winter than the summer. On the other hand, more people drive and, therefore, more gasoline is used in the summer.

Another sector of commodities is the metal sector. Of the metals, the one most frequently thought of for investing is probably gold, and this, along with silver and other precious metals, is a booming marketplace with great liquidity. Sometimes overlooked, the base metals, such as copper and steel, are essential for every growing economy for making products, and they too can make good investments, particularly with emerging nations vying for their share.

Then we come to the agricultural sector, the area where futures make most sense from a producer/consumer point of view. The farmer wishes to set a guaranteed price and be sure of a market for his or her crop, and the food processor needs the assurance of a steady expense for raw materials. However, this too is a speculative marketplace. The weather can play a significant role in the availability and pricing of crops. There are obvious seasonal cycles when growing crops. The supply of crops cannot be readily increased quickly due to the various growing cycles, so the trends tend to continue without fast reversals.

Staying on the farm, the meat markets are easily identifiable as cyclical. The growth of the animals is affected by the weather, and there are also some consumer cycles, such as the desire for more steak to barbecue in the summer. Whatever sectors are of interest, they must be followed for a time to develop an idea of what moves the prices. The trader does not need to learn how to farm and grow wheat but should have an understanding of what affects the growth and where the demand for the product comes from. This ensures future trends can be easily anticipated and profitable trades are made.

CASE STUDY: THE IMPORTANCE OF EDUCATION

Dr. Barry Burns
Founder of Top Dog Trading
www.topdogtrading.com/free_course.html

*Dr. Barry Burns is a businessperson who has owned several small companies. His business background taught him to focus on the bottom line, so his study of the financial markets was for one purpose only: to make profits. He started his study of the markets under the direction of his late father, Patrick F. Burns, who accumulated 70 years of trading experience in his lifetime. In addition, he hired three professional traders to mentor him personally and even went to Chicago to work with a former floor trader at the Chicago Mercantile Exchange. All of this research and study resulted in insights that eventually led to the development of his Top Dog Trading methodology. Dr. Burns offers a free 5-day video trading course at: **www.topdogtrading.com/free_course.html**.*

I am involved with futures and options. I prefer day trade futures over stocks because of the leverage; I can make more money faster. Of course, it is a double-edged sword, and it is possible to lose money faster, too. In fact, you can lose more than you invest. So, it is not a market for the new or inexperienced trader.

I trade options directly sometimes as well. They also have tremendous leverage, but losses are limited to the amount invested, so this is an advantage of options over futures. The downside of trading options is options do not have the same type of direct correlation with their underlying market, so they are harder to day trade. In addition, the spreads and slippage are less favorable than the futures markets I trade. My primary interest in options is as a hedge for stock positions. This is where they really shine and can be of great advantage when employed properly.

Early in my trading career, I was purely a stock trader. I was afraid of trading futures, and I did not understand options. However, I belonged to a trading club and most of the day traders in the club traded futures. They were making good money in relation to the size of their accounts, so their returns were larger than mine when I traded stocks. I hired people to teach me about futures, and I eventually became comfortable with the leverage.

To learn options, I started by reading books but was completely lost. I found options very difficult to understand. I started taking some courses and that helped a lot. With options, you have to learn new terminology and have specialized software, and there are so many other factors to consider than simply buying or selling stocks or futures. For me, there was a steep learning curve with options, and I took many classes over many years. Like many things in life, I ended up discarding most of what I learned and went back to the basics.

The current financial situation has not affected my trading at all. I am always watching various markets for opportunities — oil, real estate, currencies, gold, bonds, various industries, etc. There is always a raging bear market somewhere and always a raging bull market somewhere else. Recently, the economy was in a raging bear market followed by a raging bull market in equities. I did not trade the bear market down, but I have traded the bull market up, and it has been fantastic.

In my newsletter and blog at **www.topdogtrading.com**, I am regularly scanning the market to find these opportunities. To limit yourself to one type of market is to limit your profits unnecessarily.

Traders today can take advantage of more and varied markets than ever before through futures and options as well as other instruments. When the stock market is not moving significantly, you still have many other markets you can trade. The current financial situation has not affected my trading because I am always looking for these types of opportunities.

The thing that excites me most about futures is the leverage. I can make good money without having to commit a huge amount of my capital. With options, it is the flexibility they provide, which allows me to use them to hedge my primary positions. This is a very powerful strategy, and it is a shame more traders and investors do not take advantage of it. Hedging with options can help bring peace of mind and reduce the fear of loss for traders and investors.

The equities and futures markets have become much friendlier to the retail trader in terms of liquidity and cost. With the increased volume, lower commissions, and improvement in execution technology for the retail trader, the futures market is an amazing opportunity now for people who trade from home. The options market has also improved for the retail trader, but not as much as the futures or equities markets. The spreads and fills still leave a lot to be desired in all but the most liquid of option contracts.

I think the personal qualities that help me most at trading are patience and concentration. Many traders treat trading like a video game. They are looking for a lot of action. But my experience has been good trading is more like chess. It is important to wait for the very best, high-probability trades, and the market simply is not very generous in giving those up often. Successful traders tend to be very patient and able to concentrate for long periods of time when nothing exciting is happening. When a high probability opportunity does arrive, they have not been lulled to distraction. They are still attentive, can immediately see an opportunity as it arises, and pounce on it.

The biggest challenge I have had to face was to get the image of what I thought successful trading looked like out of my head. My original image of a successful trader was one of a person pounding out trade after trade all day long and racking up big money every hour from open to close. It was not until I hired several professional traders to work with me and watched them trade day after day that I reformulated what successful trading actually looked like. It was a complete paradigm shift, and it was a hard one to make primarily because it was not what I wanted successful trading to be.

The advice I would give to new derivatives traders is first to note that most new traders are too impatient with their individual trades, their trading day, and their trading career. Understand this business is not easy. Most people do not succeed because it is very hard — not physically, but psychologically. Most treat trading as a "get rich quick" game. I can understand because it seems like it should be easy, but it is deceptively difficult. My advice is to slow down and make a long-term commitment to it like you would any other professional career. First, become well educated and then give yourself time to get experience under your belt applying the things you learned during your education. To perfect your trading, keep a detailed trading log. If done right, this will provide your best education.

Bond Futures

Moving on to financial futures, the first to be considered is the bond future. This originated on the CBOT in 1975, first as a 30-year Treasury bond future, and the popularity of this led to many more futures contracts, including shorter maturity Treasuries such as Treasury notes.

For those unfamiliar with the operation of the markets, it may be puzzling that there are futures contracts on bonds. When first learning about stocks and bonds, common knowledge dictates that shares in a stock may go up and down and are, therefore, somewhat risky. However, bonds are loans, which may be given to the government or to a private company. Bonds pay interest and are the safer choice. If held to maturity, the bondholder gets money back, provided the company does not become insolvent. Even then, a bondholder has a better claim than a shareholder.

With that in mind, buying a futures contract on something predestined to finish at maturity at a preset value may seem unexciting, and you may feel they will not provide opportunities for profit. This is far from the case, and bonds can vary significantly in value depending on what the prevailing interest rate does. *This will be outlined later in Chapter 7*. The further away from maturity the bond is, the greater the opportunity for its value to change, and this may explain why, when futures were first issued on bonds, they started with the maximum length of bond of 30 years, which gives the greatest opportunity for variation.

A bond future is a commitment to deliver a notional bond on a future date or range of dates. The futures contract is only for an imaginary or notional bond when written and is usually settled in cash, though there are specifications for delivery if required.

The 10-year Treasury note future is popular, and as an example, here is part of the contract specification, as required by CBOT.

- **Contract size:** $100,000 face value note

- **Deliverable bonds:** U.S. Treasury notes with 6 ½ to ten years until maturity
- **Contract months:** March, June, September, and December
- **Last delivery day:** Last business day of the delivery month

There are no price limits with bond futures, so the price can vary significantly during the day.

Interest Rate Futures

Interest rate futures are a more direct futures play on the rise and fall of interest rates than the bond futures. These futures are widely used by banks and other financial institutions to hedge against changes in funding and interest rates.

One of the most popular types of interest rate futures is called the Eurodollar future. This should not be confused with the unit of currency in the European Common Market, the euro, which came into being some years after the Eurodollar future was introduced in 1981 on the CME. At the time, the Eurodollar future was the only futures contract designed from the outset to be settled in cash, though many others have now taken up this system.

Eurodollars are dollar-denominated deposits held in commercial banks outside the U.S. and are mainly based in London. The Eurodollar future traded on the CME is based on a notional $1 million three-month deposit, and the value changes every day in accordance with the expected interest rate for the period it covers. The interest rate used is the U.S. dollar LIBOR rate, set every day by British bankers. Other periods are available, shorter and longer.

The price for the Eurodollar future is not quoted in terms of the interest rate but as 100.00 minus the interest rate. For example, a futures quote of 96.40 would mean the expected interest rate for the three months of the contract is 3.60 percent (100.00 minus 3.60 equals 96.40). The minimum size or tick the contract can move is 0.01 percent. If the expected interest rate fell to 3.59 percent, the price of the futures contract would be 96.41.

To see how much a trader can gain or lose by trading these futures, simply calculate what each tick is worth. There is a notional $1 million on deposit, for three of 12 months at an annual interest rate that varies by 0.01 percent. Therefore, the value of each tick is $1,000,000 multiplied by (3/12) multiplied by (0.01/100), which equals $25.

When buying an interest rate futures contract, the trader is wagering the LIBOR rate will fall for the period of the contract or, more exactly, that the expectation of the LIBOR rate will fall. For example, if a futures contract was bought for 96.40 and the expected interest rate fell 0.1 percent. The futures contract would then be worth 96.50, and the trade would have made ten ticks profit, or $250, minus any costs. Note that it really does not matter if the rate actually fell by that much by the end of the contract, as with good timing the trader would make a profit by selling the contract when the target level was reached. That is why it is the expectation of the rate that matters, at least until the end when the rate becomes a fact.

For people interested in hedging their risk against interest rate movements, a typical use for a bank or financial house trading interest rate futures, they would be taking the other side of the deal. If the bank held $1 million on deposit and was paying interest related to the LIBOR rate to the investor, the bank could lock in the rate it would pay. Simply by selling a futures contract, the outgoings become predictable.

If the interest rate goes down, as in the example, the bank would pay less interest to the investor and would also have to pay the speculator $250 in the example. But if the interest rate went up, the additional amount the bank owed the investor would be covered by the profit made on the futures contract. If the bank does not want to take a chance on the market, it can fix its future expenditure.

Equity Futures

When equity futures are mentioned, the talk is usually of index futures, or trading on the value of one of the composite stock market indices such as the S&P 500 index, which tracks the value of the shares of 500 leading companies. Since index futures were introduced to the marketplace in the early 1980s, they have become synonymous with the futures market on stocks. Much later, in the 21st century, the futures markets have opened up to trading on single stocks; this seems to be an overlooked sector open for exploitation by savvy traders.

Index

A stock index futures contract is based on the movement of a standard stock index, and there are many different indices from which to choose. The S&P 500 is perhaps one of the most frequently traded indices, but pick the one with which you are most familiar in order to have a better feel for the direction it will move. With an index future, there is no delivery, as it would be impractical to deliver a "basket" of the index shares, so any gains or losses on the contract will be settled in cash.

S&P futures contracts are worth 250 times the value of the S&P; each full point of the index counts for $250. This makes them relatively expensive to trade, and the initial margin, though variable, can be around $20,000. The price of the contract is quoted as the index value, which is back up to about 1200 at the time of writing. As with all futures contracts, there is not one contract on the S&P 500 Index but several, each having a different settlement month.

The futures price does go up and down just as the share prices do, but they are not always moving together. This is because the futures price reflects traders' views of the market values, rather than what the values are at any particular time. If it looks like prices are going down, the futures price will probably reflect that and be less than the actual index. The price will fall because speculators will be selling the futures before the share prices drop. There are the other factors, such as cost-of-carry, which also figure into the calculation and result in it being not straightforward. However, in practice, the futures price does keep broadly in step with the market index.

One of the advantages of using an index future is diversification is already built-in. If following individual stocks, the trader would need to trade at least ten or 20 stocks in order to diversify. This leads to one way in which the index futures can be used to protect a stock portfolio.

Assume there is a significant stock portfolio and the market is hitting new highs but without good reason, so the investor is concerned there may shortly be a sell-off. If not aware of futures, the investor might be tempted to sell and take profits on the stock portfolio to protect him or herself from the consequences of the possible downturn. This could be time consuming and would keep him or her from earning the regular stock dividends he or she had become used to. Additionally, if the investor is wrong and a market correction does not happen, he or she is left with the question of when to get back into the market and will pay more costs.

An alternative would be to short a S&P 500 futures contract. As with shares, when taking a short position on a futures contract, this corresponds to a view that the value will fall. The trader effectively sells a contract and hopes for the price to go down so he or she can cover the sale by buying a contract and profit from the difference between the two prices. If the market does indeed dip, the short futures contract will make money that will compensate for the loss taken on the shares. If the market goes upward instead, the short position loses until it is covered by buying a contract, but the share values rising compensate for this. Using this technique means the investor does not get as much profit from the increasing values as would have been realized; however, if the values fall as feared, the futures contract acts as a hedge or insurance against potential losses without having to sell the portfolio.

Index futures can be used for speculation, or how a trader would use them to make money rather than just hedging their wealth. Just as with stocks, the trader would buy a contract if it seemed the value was about to go up and sell for a profit when he or she judges the best price is reached. *This will be discussed later in Chapters 11 and 12, which details constructing portfolios and trading strategies.*

Single stock futures

As mentioned before, single stock futures are an underused section of the trading market and can result in good profits once you understand them. More emphasis seems to be given to stock options in trading literature, but it is useful to have the choice of whichever derivative suits your trading situation.

Single stock futures came to the London market in 2001 when the London International Financial Futures and Options Exchange (LIFFE) — the marketplace for futures and options trading in England — introduced futures contracts on individual shares. Of necessity, these cover only the major shares, as there would not be a liquid market in many of the less traded stocks. The contract is usually for 100 shares and is cash settled, not delivered. The LIFFE contracts are traded until the third Wednesday in the specified delivery month. The CME now has similar contracts available on U.S. stocks.

The great advantage of using single stock futures rather than trading the shares is the tremendous leverage enjoyed. The other noticeable difference is the daily mark-to-market, with the possibility of getting a margin call if the value declines. This can be seen as an advantage, as it forces discipline on the trader. If a stock trader buys stocks and the price declines, it is easy to ignore this and hope they will recover. If, instead, the traders hold single stock futures, they must face the loss immediately and perhaps make the difficult decision to cut their losses and sell their interest.

Here is an example to demonstrate the leverage used with single stock futures. Imagine a trader wants to invest in British Telecom, now known as BT Group, whose shares are currently priced at around 151. Being quoted on the London market, the price is in pence and each share costs £1.50. If the trader were to buy 10,000 shares, the cost would be £15,000. Typically, to invest in 100 futures contracts, taking an interest in the same number of shares, the margin requirement would be about 10 percent of this, or £1,500.

If the price of the shares increased by 10 pence each, then the return on 10,000 shares would be £1,000. This would be nearly 7 percent for the share buyer, but for the futures buyer it would be 67 percent on his or her investment (excluding — for simplicity — any fees and charges). Single stock futures allow you to take your knowledge of individual companies and multiply your profits.

FX Futures

Similar to the forward contracts previously discussed, the FX future, or foreign currency future, is frequently used by businesses to hedge against swings in the currency exchange rates. The other side of the FX future contract might be taken by a speculator, who would anticipate making a profit from market fluctuations, or perhaps by a business based in the other country, which seeks to hedge the other way around. Instead of an individual one-off contract, as with a forward, the FX future has a standardized format, and the most active market in FX futures is at the CME in Chicago. Currency futures are actually traded at the International Monetary Market, a division of the CME, founded in 1972.

Currency futures are usually quoted as U.S. dollars for a unit of the other currency, sometimes not the way spot trades are made. Each contract is then a set amount of the other currency, for instance 125,000 euros. Delivery can be made, but usually the contracts are cash settled.

Chapter 4

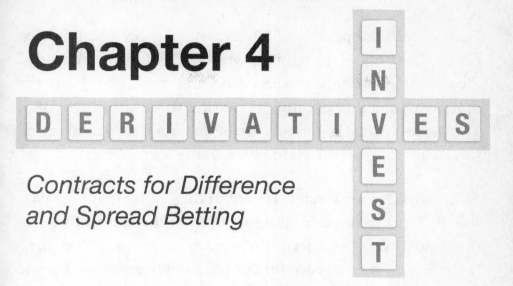

Contracts for Difference and Spread Betting

As mentioned in Chapter 1, CFDs are a fairly recent arrival to the financial scene and are proving extremely popular. They are simple to understand, easy to trade, and give the trader the ability to leverage his or her investment.

As you might expect from the name, CFDs are derivatives or financial instruments that allow the trader to profit from the difference in value of the underlying over time. They are available with many different types of underliers, including commodities, shares, currency and indices, and the trader profits by selecting an underlier that changes its value in the right direction.

One additional advantage for the trader of CFDs in the UK market is there is no stamp duty due. The United Kingdom charges stamp duty on various transactions, such as buying real estate, stocks, and shares. As CFDs do not involve owning shares, no such duty is payable.

Spread betting operates similarly, with money being made on the movement in a price without having to own any stock. The advantage of spread betting over CFDs is there is no capital gains tax due on betting winnings in the UK. The disadvantage is spreads are often larger, so you need to have a better price move to profit to the same extent.

Although CFDs are widely traded in England and Australia, the SEC, the financial regulatory body in the United States, does not currently permit them. It appears CFDs are believed to be too risky for an individual investor. CFDs are available OTC and in some listed markets, such as the Australian Securities Exchange. They can be traded in much of Europe, Australia, New Zealand, Canada, Hong Kong, Singapore, Thailand, and South Africa and are available to nonresidents in the United States.

CASE STUDY: REASONS
AND ADVICE FOR TRADING
DERIVATIVES

Daryl Guppy
CEO of Guppytraders.com
Darwin, Singapore, Beijing
www.guppytraders.com

Daryl Guppy is founder and director of Guppytraders. com Pty Ltd. Guppytraders.com is an international financial market education and training organization with offices in Darwin, Singapore, and Beijing. Guppy is a regular CNBC Asia Squawk Box technical analyst commentator, often known as "the chart man." He is recognized globally for the quality of his analysis and has a weekly CNBC.com column — Charting Asia. He actively trades equities and associated derivatives markets, including CFDs. The author of The 36 Strategies of The Chinese For Financial Traders, Trend Trading, *and seven other trading books, he has developed several leading technical indicators used by traders in stock, derivative, and currency markets. Guppy is a regular contributor for financial magazines and media in Singapore, Malaysia, China, Australia, and the United States. He oversees production of weekly analysis and trading newsletters for the Singapore/ Malaysia market, the mainland China market, and India and Australian markets. He is recognized as a leading expert on China markets. He is in demand as a speaker in Asia, China, Europe, and Australia.*

I trade contracts for difference, active warrants, index derivatives, and exchange-traded funds (ETFs).

When choosing what to trade, I look for the derivative instrument suitable for the changing market conditions. In 2008, the safest opportunities came from trading on the movements of indices. In 2009, many opportunities developed in individual stocks that had strong rally activity. These were traded with CFDs or active warrants. Increasingly, ETF trading offers a derivative solution to diversify risk and correlation risk. The objective is to select the derivative instrument most suitable for the purposes of your trade or portfolio construction.

I trade derivatives because of the limitations in portfolio risk management imposed if you trade only a single instrument, such as stocks, and the ability to magnify profits from strong trading situations that would otherwise give a lower level of return. You may observe a very reliable pattern in a stock with low volatility. Its base return is not worth trading, but if the strategy is implemented using a derivative, the return is leveraged into a better risk reward ratio.

Derivatives allow for global diversification, which reduces correlation risk. The CFD instrument gives easy global diversification without the need to open multiple brokerage accounts in different countries.

With regard to the currently evolved financial situation, the conditions of the market fundamentally changed in 2008. Many people think

2008 was an aberration. It is not. 2008 is the new trading landscape, which includes increased volatility and trend instability. Long-term trend continuity is no longer a reliable feature, so new trading systems need to be developed. Additionally, the correlated risk of exposure to a single market has been shown to increase the risk of portfolio failure. Global diversification is necessary. Derivative instruments provide a solution, which limits the risk of time exposure by increasing the profitability of short-term positions.

Additionally, derivatives allow for faster execution and reaction to the changes, which develop as "dark pool" trading is reported to markets. Derivatives help overcome problems associated with increasing opacity in market activity created by dark pool trading and settlement.

The aspect of derivatives that excites me most is the range of easily accessible opportunities coupled with leverage. However, derivatives must be traded as a derivative. They cannot be traded as a substitute for the underlying stock. What I dislike most about derivatives is leverage works in both directions. Losses are magnified quickly. This means traders must use scalping techniques in the initial derivative trade entry, and as the trade becomes profitable, they shift to long-term management. At Guppy Traders, we use our trend volatility line (TVL) management to shift from scalping to long-term position management.

Stop loss, which is the price level at which you decide to exit the trade as it is not going in the intended direction, must be based on the breakeven calculation, not the classic financial stop loss calculation. Using these would mean most trades will incur greater risk than anticipated. Using the breakeven calculation, as discussed in our TVL trading DVD, means risk is reduced. We also use momentum volatility as an entry signal and as a way of reducing the risk on entry.

The personal qualities you need in this career include having intellectual flexibility. There is not a single solution, and nor is there a solution that has been thoroughly proven. In the market, you are always operating on the edge of new work. Market conditions change, and sometimes, they change very rapidly. You must have intellectual flexibility to analyze the situation, reject outdated thinking, see new relationships, and adjust existing techniques and methods to come up with the best solution possible at the time to make a successful trade.

It is nice to be right, but it is more important to be profitable. You need discipline to follow the trade plan and the flexibility to develop new trade plans when appropriate. Deciding to stay in a losing position is not the same as developing a new trading plan. To succeed, you must focus on the process, not the result. Worry about executing and managing the trade correctly. The money will follow.

The biggest success I have had in derivatives was taking significant profits in 2008 by trading from the long side using index derivatives. The most significant challenge I have had to face is to adjust stop loss methods. This is followed by the need for understanding trend volatility rather than price volatility. And third, to accept you are trading the derivative, and this is not a substitute for the underlying stock. When I trade the derivative, I am trading the derivative. I do not assess the derivative behavior against the performance of the underlying. You must trade what you see, not what you believe or hope.

If I was to give advice to someone who wanted to succeed in trading derivatives, I would say you need to survive in order to grow. You need to learn and master those trading strategies good for your size. You need to develop survival strategies suited to your size in the market. The private trader has a tremendous capacity for self-delusion. Many beginners assume they ought to follow and imitate large professional traders. They accept the investment objectives of Warren Buffet can also be theirs. We vaguely understand these objectives as being to consistently make money over a long period, with occasional satisfying and very successful trades. Do not confuse the activities and image of professional traders with success, and do not try to imitate their behavior, hoping success will follow. You do not need to imitate the methods of institutional traders. There are important differences between you and them. Before you enter the water as a private trader, know who you are and, just as importantly, what you are not.

What is the difference between you and Warren Buffet? What is the difference between a trader working on the floor for Morgan Stanley and working for you? These questions are not trivial. Your answers determine your trading techniques and, even more importantly, your money management techniques. Mutual funds and institutional traders make your money work for them. Your challenge is to make money work for you.

Understand this first, and risk control, money management, method, and trade discipline will follow. When you have developed good equity trading skills in short-term time periods, then you can transfer those skills to the derivative markets. Be prepared to learn new skills and methods in these new market areas.

When CFDs were first invented, they were used by institutional and hedge fund investors. It was several years before they became available and known to individual traders. They have the advantage of trading on margin, which means the investment is leveraged perhaps ten times. To set against this, you are charged interest for the margin for the time you hold the position in the CFDs. This means CFDs are best regarded as short-term trading instruments rather than investments.

As CFDs allow you to profit from a change in price, it is just as easy to short a stock to profit from a fall in value as it is to go long and profit from an increase in price. In this way, an investor could hedge against a temporary fall in value of his or her shareholding by taking out a short CFD.

There are other advantages for those traders able to use CFDs. As they are available in many markets and on many underliers, one brokerage account for CFDs allows a trader to take an interest in commodities, stocks, foreign exchange, and many other financial instruments. The costs of trading are also low, and some CFD trades are not charged a commission because the broker will make a profit from the spread between the buy and sell price.

It is estimated the CFD market is second only to the forex market in the amount of daily turnover. It is highly liquid with an estimated $2 trillion changing hands every day. Despite this, the CFD market allows you to start trading with as little as $100.

The spread-betting market is smaller and depends on the bookmakers to set prices and provide liquidity. For short holding periods of a few days up to a week or two, it may be considered the better way of trading, but CFDs will usually work out to be more cost effective when you are considering holding them for months at a time. CFDs are useful up to three months, after which the financing costs become more noticeable, and you need to balance the costs of the alternative of direct stock ownership. Because of the commonalities to CFDs, spread betting is not discussed in detail separately, as the points made are generally applicable to both forms.

Commodities and Precious Metals CFDs

Ask any trader about commodities, and it is natural for them to assume you are referring to futures contracts. In any market where CFD trading is permitted, you will find they have some advantages over using futures.

First, to trade in many different sectors and securities, you only need one account. Your CFD broker should be able to provide access to all the different markets available. When trading CFDs, you always have a choice of whether to go long or short, so enjoy ultimate flexibility in choosing your trades.

CFDs in commodities are available for all the markets, which are traded on futures contracts. That includes agricultural products such as grain and livestock, energy products such as oil and gas, and precious metals such as gold and silver. You can also trade in overseas markets as easily as in your home market because of the way that CFDs are organized.

The pricing for commodity CFDs is based on the futures market, taken to the nearest month, and the CFD will be rolled over into the next contract when each month expires. As CFDs are always cash settled, there is no possibility you will take delivery of the underlying, as there is when trading futures. When the CFD rolls into the next month contract, there may be an adjustment on your account to compensate.

As with futures, CFDs are always marked-to-market each day, so there will be minor fluctuations in your account on a daily basis, and you may receive a margin call from your broker if the market turns against you. Occasionally, some brokers will not automatically roll the contract over to the next month but will provide a cash settlement instead. Usually these brokers will also ask you if you would like the contract manually rolled over.

Because they are similar to futures contracts, you may be wondering about the benefits of trading CFDs. There are advantages that may tip the balance for you, provided you are in a country that allows CFD trading.

Often the margin requirement for CFD trading is less than for futures, and it may be as little as 5 percent. This means you either need less money for the quantity you want to trade or you can trade larger quantities for the same amount. The margin rate, which is the interest charged for trading on margin, will probably be about the same as is charged for futures contracts, so there is little difference between the two for this expense.

Significant benefits can be found in selecting the quantity and trading periods you want. If you do not want to be involved in the larger quantities standard for futures contracts, the CFD is a great advantage. Commodities CFDs are usually traded on smaller quantities than the standard futures contracts amounts. Often, the amount of the commodity is "one unit," in which the unit used depends on the commodity involved. For example, a CFD for oil may be based on one barrel, and a CFD for gold would be based on one ounce. Occasionally you will find some brokers insist on a certain minimum amount, such as 25 barrels of oil. Check on this when selecting a broker if it is important to you.

The other disadvantage with a futures contract, which does not arise with the CFD, is futures are settled on a certain day of the month. As mentioned above, CFDs may be affected in value by the futures settlement date, but you can hold your trade open until the day you want. The only point to note in this respect is that CFDs are better for trading than investing because of the interest charged, so you will probably not want to hold the contract more than a month.

Equity CFDs

Equity CFDs also have all the advantages of leverage when dealing with the stock market. A typical stockbroker may allow a margin of 50 percent, but a CFD broker may require only 10 percent of the share value you want to trade. Therefore, you need much less money to participate in the profits of a share price rise, or with the same amount of money, you can control far more shares. Although the SEC does not permit CFDs for U.S. residents, traders in other markets can find CFDs based on worldwide stock markets, including London, Europe, and the U.S. markets.

Although there is no actual share ownership, avoiding taxes and duties for the UK trader, holding an equity CFD is similar to owning the shares. For example, when a dividend is due, the holder of a long CFD position will receive a credit for it. Sometimes, there are minor deductions for tax and administration, but the credit will be about 90 percent of the declared dividend.

If the trader has taken a short position in the CFD, then the opposite applies. The trader's account will be debited by the amount of the dividend. Another difference from owning shares is the holder of the CFD has no voting rights at the shareholder's meeting. Ownership of the shares never changes hands — an essential point of the CFD structure.

Once again, the CFD trader should expect to see daily fluctuations in his or her account. The holding will be marked-to-market each day, and this may result in a margin call. If the trade is going the right way, then additional funds will be credited to the account, which could be used for trading.

Compared to owning the stocks, you will notice there is a daily maintenance or interest charge. Consequently, if you are looking at a long-term holding, CFDs would not be a suitable trading vehicle. With CFDs, you are looking for a price change within the following month at the most

When you look at the advantages of trading CFDs compared with single stock futures, they are similar to those mentioned in the previous section on commodities. Namely, there is no set time limit or expiry date, which gives you greater flexibility in trading. Also, subject to your broker, you are not restricted in the lot size and may even be able to trade on one share. With single stock futures, you need to trade in lots of 100 shares.

Sector CFDs

Often when trading stocks the concept of market sectors comes up. This idea divides commercial businesses into groups of similar products called sectors. For instance, the energy sector would include companies involved in gas, electricity, and oil, and the transportation sector would cover trains and buses. The idea of market sectors is valuable, as it goes through cycles, and sometimes, one sector is better for the trader than another.

There are many sectors to choose from, and sector CFDs are available to allow trading in whichever area seems to offer the most promise. Sectors include finance, energy, retail, technology, health, and others. By trading sector CFDs, you are able to trade in a way that would be difficult if you were limited to trading stocks.

When you trade a sector CFD instead of individual stocks, the sector will tend to average the volatility of the stocks in the sector and provide diversification. This is particularly advantageous if the sector is in a growth mode but you are uncertain which of the companies in the sector will succeed.

You do not always have to look for a growth sector of the market. It is just as easy to trade CFDs short by betting on a decline in the underlying. For instance, if you felt the retail trade would be taking a hit during Christmas, you would be able to trade in that direction and profit from a loss of value in the sector.

One disadvantage, sometimes cited with sector CFDs, is the spreads between the bids and ask prices — the prices at which to buy and sell the CFDs — tend to be quite large. This means you need a correspondingly larger move in the market in order to break even before you can start counting your profit. Because you are paying interest charges the longer you hold onto the CFDs, this can be a delicate balance. Generally, you will find the spread is smaller when trading equity CFDs.

As a sector CFD represents a basket of shares, you may find you benefit from the issue of dividends on those shares with your account credited for nearly the full value. If you have gone short on the CFD, you will unfortunately find your account is debited in the amount of the dividends. There are different market makers for sector CFDs, and you may find some variation between the offerings from different brokers.

Although sector CFDs have advantages, it may be worth comparing the costs of trading equities CFDs instead. If looking at a sector where there is a dominant company or two, it may make more sense to trade the equity CFDs in those companies and enjoy the lower spreads for greater profit.

Sector CFDs can be combined with each other or with equity trades to provide a more sophisticated method of trading. For example, in a technique called "pairs trading," you might decide health care will do better than technology in the near future. In this case, buy long sector CFDs in health care and short CFDs in the technology sector. The advantage of this approach is it does not matter how the economy in general performs. As long as health care outperforms technology, whether by growth or by performing less badly than technology, you will secure a profit.

An alternative plan is to identify a company in a certain market sector you think will outperform the other companies, perhaps because it is innovative or has superior management. Again, the strategy is to separate individual performance from the general economy. In this case, you could go long with equity CFDs in the company and short on the sector CFDs. Whatever the sector as a whole does, provided the company you have selected is indeed superior, you have guaranteed your profit.

Index CFDs

There are countless indices in the financial markets. The most well known in the United States are the Dow Jones Industrial Average, also called the Dow, the NASDAQ 100, and the S&P 500. In London, there is the FTSE 100 and 250; in Australia, the Aussie 200; and Germany has the DAX 30. These indices have been assembled to give a quick indication of the overall health of any particular market and are made up of shares values in the market, with the number in the name corresponding to the number of companies included.

Regardless of location, you can trade CFDs that track many of these worldwide indices. Trading an index allows you to take a view on the overall economy of a particular country or financial market. Remembering you can trade "short" as easily as "long" with CFDs, whether you think an economy will boom or tank, you can position yourself to profit from the move.

Index CFDs will offer better leverage than equity CFDs. Typically, the margin will only be 5 percent. It is not usual to be charged a commission on index CFDs, as the broker will achieve his or her profits from the two or three points spread between the bid and ask prices.

Again, one of the greatest advantages of trading an index CFD compared with an index future is you are not limited to trading the larger size lots required for futures and do not have set expiry dates.

You can trade index of CFDs in pairs, in a similar way to that explained in sector CFDs. In this case, assume you believe the London stock market will outperform the U.S. market. Whether the global market as a whole was buoyant or in recession would become irrelevant if you went long on the FTSE index CFD and short on the Dow Jones index CFD. If your belief in the British market being stronger was correct, you would still profit from placing this strategy.

Currency CFDs

Currency, or FX, CFDs have become popular in recent years, perhaps because of the increase in regular forex trading over the Internet. Although FX trading is not complex, with just a handful of currency pairs accounting for the majority of the action, FX CFDs make the process even easier.

In common with the FX market, trading currency CFDs allows significant leverage of the trading capital. The forex market is highly efficient, and currencies can be easily traded either way. For instance, you can be long or short on the U.S. dollar versus the euro depending how you see the market progressing. The advantage of using CFDs to trade in currency is you are not stuck with the standard lot sizes, which may be larger than you wish to use.

Less than 5 percent of the contracts traded on the FX market are intended to convert currency, and the remainder is speculative. Because CFDs are always traded for the difference and are cash settled, there is no doubt you are trading for the difference in value and not for the currency. Being able to choose the amount traded can be an advantage if you wish to take up several positions in the market or are undercapitalized.

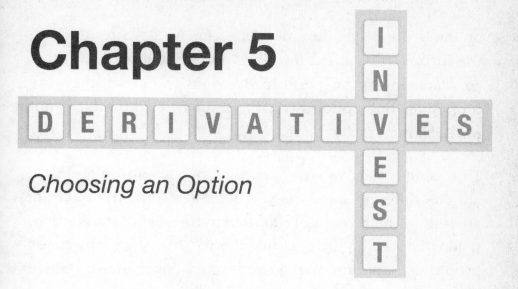

Chapter 5

Choosing an Option

In the field of derivatives, options have a special place and are widely employed for speculative trading. They are similar to, but significantly different from, futures contracts, and each form of derivative has its advantages and disadvantages. As indicated earlier in the outline of options, there are several terms used in describing option contracts, which can add to their mystique or confusion, and they are common to options contracts on different underliers.

Options are simple in concept, and once that is understood thoroughly, the additional features can be easily assimilated. Buying an option gives the buyer a right to buy or sell something at a future date for a price set now. Given the unpredictability of the future, this results in significant profit if the right option is chosen. The biggest difference from using futures for speculation is with options, the buyer has no obligation to go through with the future transaction if it does not make money. Futures contracts must be performed, whether or not they are profitable, but options contracts may be forgotten if not worth using or exercising.

This single fact makes the way people speculate with options different from the use of futures. For the buyer of an option, their losses are limited to the cost of that option, paid when the contract is taken out. This is the way many people use options, using the limited downside to reduce their risk and hoping to select the right choices to realize the upside profit.

Another side to option trading is not so clear-cut but also has great opportunities for profit. For every options contract sold, someone stands behind the contract, receives the payment, and is required to satisfy the deal if the option makes a profit. This person is called the "option writer," and being in this position, the option writer can also make good money if he or she is careful about what they do. The requirement to satisfy the option contract is not much different from being on the wrong side of a futures contract, and each time someone writes an option, they get paid, which is money kept free and clear, regardless of whether the option finishes in the money.

An option offers the flexibility that the buyer or holder does not have to take up the option if it does not suit or make a profit. That is the reason the option costs money, as the buyer pays for the privilege of having a choice. Contrast this to the position on a futures contract where, at the time of taking the contract, each party has a neutral financial position.

Note that options are basically a "zero sum" trade. Whatever one trader makes, the other trader must lose. The great advantage of options over buying and selling shares is it requires a much smaller investment to have control of, and profit from, the change in the price of shares when you have an option contract.

As options give the trader choices, there are a range of options to purchase at various prices. An option almost always covers 100 shares, but there is a choice of the month of expiration (from those available) and the amount paid per share if the option is in profit. Not all prices are available, and, for the most part, the share price rises in $5 increments.

Each of the available options will have a different purchase price. If the option is "out of the money" and far from the current or spot price, the likelihood the option will make money is slight, and you can expect to pay little for it. If the price is close or even in profit already, the option will cost a lot more. *Costs and pricing will be discussed further in Chapter 8.*

American/European Styles

There are two distinct styles of options, the American option and the European option, and the difference between the two is important. The European option is more restrictive, and the American gives more choice.

The European option gives the buyer the right to exercise it on the expiration date. If the option is "in the money" on that day, meaning the price named in the option is better than the market price, it will be exercised and make a profit. It does not matter what has happened in the intervening days since the option was bought; the only concern is the underlying prices on the last day.

In contrast, the American style of option can be exercised whenever the buyer wants to up until the expiration. If it is "in the money" the day after it is bought, the option buyer can take the profit and close the option. This does mean the buyer must decide whether to take the profit on the table or hold on to the option hoping it will gain more value. The option can only be exercised once, so if the trader decides to take an early profit by exercising the option, any later price moves do not matter. *Exercising an option early is discussed further in Chapter 12.*

The style of option does not always follow from where the option is bought. Many options available around the world are American style, but not all. Some cash-settled index options are European style, as are some OTC options. American options, having more flexibility and intrinsically more chance of allowing a profit to be taken by judicious exercising, can usually be expected to cost more. Another style that is rarely come across is called a Bermudan option, a compromise between the two styles. It allows the option to be exercised before the expiration date but only on certain days, such as one day per week.

The Jargon

The price of the option is the "premium" the option buyer pays for the contract. The buyer is also referred to as the "option holder," which is the opposite of the "option writer" who takes the premium and must fulfill the contract if required to do so by the option holder.

The option contract itself has a price, called a "strike price," at which the option holder can buy or sell the underlying. There is also a date, the "expiration date," by which time the option must be taken up or expire.

If the option gives the holder the opportunity to buy the underlying, a "long position," the option is known as a "call" option. The holder can "call" for the delivery of the underlying at the agreed strike price. If the option gives the holder the right to sell the underlying at the strike price, it is called a "put" option; effectively the holder can "put" the underlying with the writer and receive money for it. This would be a "short position."

When the option holder decides to buy or sell the underlying, this is called "exercising" the option. The option writer who must comply is said to be "assigned" the task, and this comes from the exchange-traded options where the exchange literally chooses a writer who will sell or buy the underlier in accordance with the option contract. Even so, the actual delivery of the shares and money is handled by the exchange to ensure there is no chance of defaulting on the contract.

If exercising the option would not make a profit, the option is "out of the money." An option where the strike price is the same as the spot price is called "at the money," and an option in profit is called "in the money." Note that a European style option can be "in the money" but still not make a profit in the end, if the spot price changes against you before the expiration date.

The other point to note is if the option is at the money, this does not mean the option holder has broken even on the deal. The premium paid means the spot price must go over the option price for a long option by a certain margin in order to break even. The required amount over depends on the premium paid, which can vary from day to day depending when the option was bought.

Equity Options

The simplest type of option, the equity or stock option, uses stock in a single company as an underlier. If a trader buys a call option and the stock goes up in value, it will come into profit. With a put option, the trader is looking for a fall in share price in order to enter the profit zone. Exactly how much the stock price must increase or fall depends on the strike price of the option bought and the current spot price of the stock.

Equity options are usually exchange-traded, and thus, contract performance is guaranteed by the exchange. Some options are available OTC, and these include some of the smaller shares not listed on the exchanges.

Equity options are almost always physically settled and not cash settled. This means, if exercised, the holder of a call option will receive the shares at the agreed option price, and the holder of a put option can sell the shares and receives payment. Each option traded is for 100 shares, so the total price paid or received is 100 times the value in the option contract.

A profit can be taken any time it is available before the expiration date simply by selling the option back to the exchange. It is not necessary to exercise the option to close out the trade. Options can be readily traded, and if the option purchased becomes more valuable over time, it can be sold before the expiration.

CASE STUDY: OPTIONS & SELF-DISCOVERY

Brian McAboy
Founder of InsideOutTrading.com
www.insideouttrading.com

Successful and consistent trading can be a daunting challenge. Brian McAboy helps individual traders simplify the business of trading and effectively overcome the obstacles often encountered. McAboy created InsideOutTrading.com, where traders come for real help with their trading. Benefit from the free reports and videos at www.insideouttrading.com.

I trade options in the commodities markets. I prefer this type because of the built-in risk limits when buying (automatic risk management, albeit minimum) in addition to stops. Plus, it just fits well with longer-term trading. In my opinion, options are a good place for beginners; plus, once you have developed more, there are a myriad of ways a trader can be creative to gain further advantage and decrease risk.

Options are where I started, and they were just easy to grasp and have seemed to be the best fit of all I have tried. Day trading forex was fun, but it was too easy to get totally consumed, and stocks did not have the kind of return I wanted, particularly for the time spent. Futures markets have always been more to my liking.

The current financial situation has not affected me much, except in dealing with a bit more negativity in the general climate. That is one of the great things about trading: The climate does not matter if you know what you are doing. In fact, times like these are when it can be easy to rack up some incredible gains — again if you are savvy.

What excites me most about derivatives is being able to get in on trades out of the money; it is like buying prime real estate at a steep discount. I think being a quality engineer has been a significant help by allowing me to have the focus of business and processes plus the quality tools to apply to trading. The other major personal quality that has assisted me is that I pursue being good at whatever I do, and trading is definitely a field where excellence is rewarded.

The biggest success I have had in derivatives was getting to the point where it did not matter if I was on the sidelines or missed a winning trade. Just to finally have that peace and confidence that all is well and that the opportunities are abundant was a wonderful milestone to reach. The biggest challenge I have had to face was the self-discovery process trading will put you through. You can start off in trading thinking you know yourself inside and out, but you soon learn many things about yourself, such as how you view the world, how you handle different situations, what your real beliefs are, and how mentally tough you are. Trading will enlighten you to many things you otherwise would never learn, each a worthwhile lesson if you pay attention to it.

I would advise someone who is starting off in derivatives to do the personal explorations before you start actively trading. Ask questions of yourself before you even select a style or strategy. Too many traders do it backwards: They get busy and let the markets direct them to the introspections.

The other most important item is to have a real and functional business plan. Trading is a real business and, in most respects, no different from most other businesses, including the failure rate and reasons for failure. If you take the time to build your trading business on paper beforehand, you give yourself a tremendous advantage and dramatically increase your chances of success.

Index Options

Index options are similar to stock options, but as with futures, it is impractical to give physical delivery, so they are cash settled. No shares ever change hands. Index options allow diversification into the market as a whole and represent a leveraged way to profit from an upturn in the economy. Against this advantage, the disadvantages are that a premium must be paid for the option contract and that the contract will run out of time at the expiration date. If the stocks had been bought, there would still be a profit made if the upturn was delayed by a month or two, whereas the option may expire worthless before this comes about.

Commodity Options

In the agricultural sector, as previously explained, producers can sell futures contracts, which guarantee the price they will sell their produce for at a future date. As farming is sometimes unpredictable, some users are not prepared to make a commitment in fear of a bad harvest. To cope with this need, commodity options were introduced.

A commodity option is not actually an option to buy or sell a physical commodity, but an option to buy or sell a futures contract on a commodity. This allows the agricultural sector the freedom to buy "insurance" that any crops will be sold at a good price without committing to the fullest possible production. For the price of the premium, the option buyer can ensure the crops or products produced can be sold at a prearranged and satisfactory price without having to guess the production levels in advance and perhaps overcommit.

Currency Options

A currency, or FX, option gives the holder the right but not the obligation to exchange two currencies in the future at a predetermined rate. These are available in the European style, with the exchange happening on a set date, or the American style, where the exchange can take place any time up until the expiration date.

Exchange-traded currency options are standardized, and OTC options can be individually negotiated for specific circumstances. As the physical underlier in this type of option is another currency, each option contract encompasses a right to buy a currency and a right to sell another currency. In effect, they include a call option and a put option (for the other currency) in one trading vehicle.

Currency options are widely used by many financial undertakings, banks, and corporations. They are a hedging tool, which can guard against adverse moves in the currency exchange rate for a future transaction. In this way, they are similar in application to the currency futures. The advantage of a currency option is, if the currency exchange rate moves in the business's favor, it does not have to be used, and the business may make more profit. The disadvantage is a premium must be paid, and whether or not the option becomes in the money, the payment will detract from the profit made.

There are many other ways in which currency options may be applied. For the speculator, they present a limited-risk way of speculating on the moves of the foreign exchange market. For the investor in foreign stocks, they are used to avoid the risk associated with currency fluctuations before taking a profit.

The ways in which derivatives can be combined to minimize the disadvantage of paying a premium will be discussed later in Chapter 12.

Interest Rate Options

Interest rate derivatives have already been considered in this text when discussing the forward rate agreement and the interest rate futures. These are used to hedge against adverse moves in the interest rate during the life of the contract, or they can be used for speculation and profit. In the discussion of derivative types in Chapter 1, swaps were mentioned, and the idea of swapping a fixed interest rate payment with a floating rate payment was outlined. All these previous derivatives have one thing in common: The initial rates are agreed so both parties to the contract feel at the outset that the rates are fair, and it is not costing them to enter the deal. The contracts give security in the amount of payments regardless of fluctuations, but neither party started out believing he or she was paying for the privilege and each considered the deal financially neutral.

With an interest rate option, in contrast to futures and forwards, the scales are tilted. If no premium was paid, the holder of the option would have an unfair position, as the option would only give a positive outcome or expire worthless. That is why the premium represents the cost of attaining that position and summarizes the market's sympathy toward the various outcomes.

Interest rate options may be OTC or exchange-traded and provide another way of managing interest rate risk, reducing the exposure to unforeseen fluctuations. Essentially, a European-style interest rate option is a call option for a forward rate agreement (FRA). Instead of having the downside of the FRA, the buyer of the option can let the option expire worthless. If the interest rate goes against the buyer by the expiration date, the payment is made to compensate in the same way as with an FRA.

Binary Options

Binary options are perhaps the simplest derivatives you can find. In some ways, they are simply a form of betting. The name binary may imply a simple two-state function, such as on-off, and in this case the two states are you win and get paid, or you lose and get nothing.

Devotees of binary options throw scorn on the complications of traditional options, which many regard as too complex, particularly when you get to strategies that combine several trades in the same concept. Binary options require only that you have an opinion of whether the market is going up or down and are prepared to back this opinion by making a trade.

Unlike traditional options, there are no calculations to be done on the possible future value. When you make the trade, you know the two possible outcomes precisely. The winning payout is fixed for the particular trade by the broker, and a losing trade returns nothing. Typically, binary options are over in a short period, sometimes expiring on an hourly basis, but certainly not staying open more than a few days.

The broker must make his or her assessment of the chances it will go up or down and then sets the payouts accordingly. The sum of the payouts either way will be a little less than the stake, and this is where the broker makes money.

To make a trade, you will need a binary options trading account, different from a regular options account. You may trade on indices or major stocks. Not all securities are available to trade, but the ones with the highest trading volume should be listed.

Because of the simple system, it does not matter how much the index or price moves. The only thing that matters is whether it goes up or down. If it moves one cent or five dollars, the payouts are the same: nothing if you guess wrong, or the amount the broker told you when you placed the trade if your selection is correct.

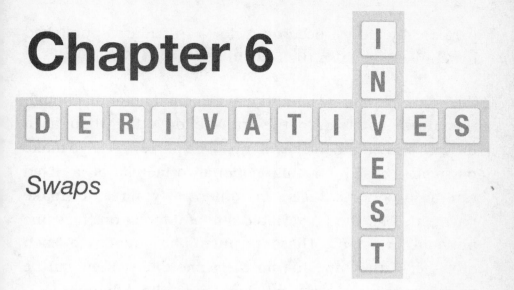

Chapter 6

DERIVATIVES

Swaps

S waps are contracts in which the two parties agree to exchange payments in the future. The payments are based on two different factors, and neither party knows which will be detrimental and which beneficial, but they are prepared to exchange the values for their own reasons, such as their views on the markets or the economy. Inevitably, the swap is financially neutral at the outset; otherwise, the disadvantaged party would not freely enter into it. Often, a series of payments are involved. Swaps are frequently OTC transactions because of the variety of circumstances that may lead to the contract.

Interest Rate Swaps

As discussed in Chapter 1 as an example of swap contracts, a common form of swap is the exchanging of fixed rate and floating rate interest payments. The floating rate is periodically reset according to a standard published benchmark, such as the LIBOR.

This type of swap has a notional principal amount, though this never enters into the transaction other than as a means to calculate the payments. One party agrees to make payments based on this notional principal at a fixed rate on a periodic basis. The other party agrees to make payments based on a variable rate of interest on the same notional principal. These payments are made to each other, or if they are due on the same dates, they can be netted out so one party only has to pay the difference.

It may be one party to the swap contract knows he or she will have to pay a greater amount at the start of the contract. However, the individual would only agree to this if he or she thought recovering the difference later as the floating interest rate changed was a possibility. The key to an interest rate swap is both parties to the contract estimate they are no worse off by taking part in it and want the change of terms it brings.

Equity Swap

An equity swap involves an agreement to swap cash flows where at least one of the sets of payments depends on the value of shares or a share portfolio. Typically, this may happen when a shareholder wants to monetize or receive cash for the shares but still wants to benefit from any change in value of the shares over a set period. It may even include paying dividends due. This arrangement is called a "total return" deal.

The other payment leg can be negotiated to be, for example, a key reference interest rate. One party to the deal would receive payments as if the shares were still owned, whereas the other party would receive a notional interest payment. Equity swaps are OTC and are useful tools for companies, investment houses, and banks.

An example of how they are used would be with an investor who wants to invest in foreign shares but is restricted from doing so or has limitations associated with such actions. The investor would find a swap dealer prepared to take on the swap and provide the returns on a set collection of shares in exchange for a regular interest payment, which, in this case, would be related to the notional capital needed to purchase the shares.

The dealer would happily take on this contract, as he or she could borrow the money to actually invest in the shares, which would service the interest on the loan from part of the investor's interest payments. The deal could be arranged so payments were all made in dollars to avoid further complication. Whether the dealer would actually buy the shares would depend on his or her view of the market and propensity for risk, but the fact there is a reasonable means to hedge the transaction makes it a viable deal.

Similarly, it is possible for a company to take out an equity index swap and receive payments in accordance with the moving of a recognized index of shares, such as the S&P 500, and again paying interest tied to a publicized rate plus premium based on the overall value of the shares.

Credit Default Swap

The credit default swap is different from the derivatives this book has discussed so far. All the previous derivatives have involved incremental financial risk, whether it is a change in the rate of currency exchange or a stock price rising to above a strike price. The credit default swap is the financial market's attempt to quantify in a price the chance of a debtor defaulting on a debt.

Looked at in one way, it is a difficult exercise, as the debt may or may not be repaid. Therefore, putting a price on it may seem to be, at best, a guessing game, and the outcome is either one case or the other. However, when this concept is analyzed, it is no different from taking out insurance against an eventuality that may never occur. All the credit default swap has as a basis is an estimate of the chance of a default, which the premium can be based on.

Credit default swaps are often used to cover mortgages, municipal bonds, and company debts. The buyer of the credit default swap is protected against losses from a default, or inability to pay, on the part of the mortgage holder or other money borrower. The seller of the credit default swap guarantees payment will be made as it should, whether or not the borrower is sound.

If this sounds familiar, it may be because one of the major financial problems in recent times arose because of the use of credit default swaps. It is easy to see why a bank would want to use credit default swaps to cover its lending. Once a contract is in place, it can count the money it has lent on its books as certain to be repaid, and this increases its capitalization and allows further lending to take place. This is one way banks make money.

The concept of credit default swaps seems good and was a clever invention by the executives of JPMorgan to mitigate the risk burdening their company and forcing huge reserves to be held rather than used to generate more income. One problem with the practice of credit default swaps, however, is there was not enough legislation to provide safeguards against things going wrong.

Credit default swaps are privately negotiated contracts, and no one really knows what values are at stake at any time. The insurance giant, AIG, was bailed out of $14 billion worth of swaps by the government, and this literally saved many other institutions from disaster. If AIG had been declared bankrupt and defaulted on these insurance contracts, many more companies would not be able to continue operation. Some say the total market was more than $60 billion.

Although they have similarities to insurance, credit default swaps do have differences. One is the regulation is not in place to make sure the company selling the swaps has sufficient means to make good if the swaps are called in to cover the debts. Warren Buffett is one of the world's most successful investors and was ranked by Forbes magazine as the world's richest man in 2008, with a net worth of approximately $62 billion. He has called credit default swaps "financial weapons of mass destruction." He was nearly proved correct in this by the use of credit default swaps on baskets of subprime mortgages and risky emerging markets, which contributed to the financial crisis of 2008.

With this said, and the benefit of hindsight, there are constructive uses for credit default swaps that do not threaten the fabric of the financial industry. As with many derivatives, they can be used in several ways — for hedging, speculation, and arbitrage. The reduction in risk by hedging with credit default swaps is obvious and may have significant advantages for the buyer of the swap. Speculation is to take on risk in the expectation of higher returns, and the seller of the credit default swap or protection takes this position, risking for the expectation of gain. It is up to the seller to take a responsible position in determining the risk they are taking on, to charge an appropriate amount, and to know how they will fulfil the contract if payment is required.

Currency Swaps

Sometimes, the two parties taking part in an interest rate swap want to do it in different currencies, and this is where a cross-currency interest rate swap, or simply "currency swap," is used. In this case, the parties want to hedge against interest rate variations but are not concerned about making or losing money from possible currency fluctuations. As discussed in Chapter 3, other derivatives, such as FX futures, can be used to profit from correctly anticipating the movements of the currency exchange rates. The interest rates can be fixed or floating.

The main difference with currency swaps is in the treatment of the notional principal. In a single currency interest rate swap, there is no need for the capital on which the interest payments are based to actually change hands, and it is merely used for the calculations. To avoid the effect of an exchange rate variation with a currency swap, the principal does change hands for the duration of the contract and is handed back, unchanged, at the end. This means both parties avoid having to take on the risk of losing some principal over the duration of the contract.

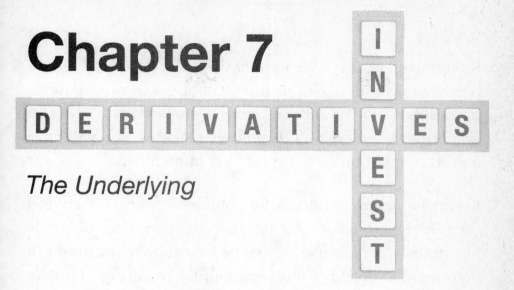

Chapter 7

DERIVATIVES

The Underlying

H aving gone over the many different ways in which derivatives can operate together with some examples of practical uses, it is time to consider in detail what the underlying or physical goods consist of. The mechanics of the derivatives depend on the actions of the underlying, and a good understanding will mean you are better able to anticipate the actions of the derivatives.

Commodities

Commodities are physical goods, grown or manufactured. Some are processed and all are shipped. The futures market began when growers and buyers realized contracts for these items reduced their risks and gave assurance of supply, which allowed trading to continue smoothly.

Energy

Energy commodities are frequently in the news and have a record of volatility, with dramatic changes in price caused by supply and demand and international events. If you can understand what drives the energy markets, you will have a good foundation for a career in trading futures.

It can be assumed oil is the commodity most discussed on the energy front and has been the subject of many headlines. The producers, typified by the Organization of Petroleum Exporting Countries (OPEC), readily manipulate its supply. OPEC was formed 50 years ago, initially to resist pressure from the consuming countries for a reduction in the price of oil, but the group came to the public's attention in 1973 when, for political reasons, the price of oil was increased dramatically and output was cut. This was the start of the immense wealth oil producing countries have enjoyed. The members of OPEC have not always seen eye-to-eye on policies but can exert a powerful force on the markets.

Although supply can be readily adjusted, the demand, intrinsic to Western civilization, is not so easily assuaged, and even when the price of gasoline soars in the United States, consumption is only marginally reduced. Rising oil prices affect most areas of modern life, as prices are increased to cover additional transportation costs and manufacturing costs.

As a result, rising oil prices usually reduce sales in all sectors and often lead to a problem for the Federal Reserve

Bank whose mission is to stabilize the economy. The Fed is in control of interest rates but only has this one major tool to regulate the economy. If they reduce the interest rates, this eases the burden on the consumer and stimulates the economy. On the other hand, stimulating the economy may fuel inflation, which will already be rising with the increased prices caused by the oil. On balance, the Fed will often raise interest rates to discourage the expenditure on more expensive oil. Inflation is normally considered more of a threat than recession.

There are other factors that need to be addressed when discussing oil. For instance, beyond a doubt, oil removed from the ground is not being replaced, which means the oil resources will run out. Crude oil takes a long time, eons in fact, to be created, and our rate of usage allows no replenishment. Exploration and development of new techniques means the prospect of oil running out has receded from the public mind, but it is no less obvious that someday it will happen.

Some evidence of the dwindling supply has already been seen. Reduction in oil reserves held by the big oil companies has already taken place. In fact, reserves held by the big three — Exxon Mobil, Chevron, and ConocoPhillips — have fallen by 6 percent from 2005 to 2008. Even Exxon Mobil is only replacing about 75 percent of its annual production. What this means for the trader is the market for oil is sensitive to any news of production problems or solutions, political factors, and other matters.

The price moves vigorously, making this a great market to be involved in if you can keep up with the developments.

In addition to action in the crude oil market, the heating oil, petroleum, and natural gas markets are active and subject to seasonal variations. The cycles of use during the year are obvious. For example, you may not want to go long on heating oil when spring arrives, as there is likely to be less demand in the warmer months, but the cycles cannot be relied upon to necessarily affect individual contract prices, only to indicate the overall trend.

Agricultural

One of the oldest futures markets, agricultural is less popular for trading now, perhaps because of the inevitable heavy dependence on the uncontrollable and unpredictable weather variations. This does mean the market can be volatile, but it is less yielding to analysis. There are several grain markets actively traded. Corn is important and has received increased attention in recent years due to the possibility of making ethanol from the corn supply — an idea that has upset the food markets but may have a small long-term effect. Wheat and soybeans are also staples of the commodity trader.

A little historic research will show how the seasons affect the values of these commodities. The trader in crops needs to know the growing seasons and how bad weather can affect the crop. For instance, does a late frost destroy the entire crop or only part of it, and how does this vary with the geographical regions? Although standardized contracts do not usually include the area of origin of the crop, with research the trader can determine which areas are harvested at what time and which contracts will be affected.

For the trader prepared to stay on top of this amount of information, agricultural commodity futures can be profitable. Unless brought up in an agricultural community, traders would be well advised to study the basics so they can develop their understanding of the finer points.

Other basics include the fact that the supply is the more variable factor in the supply-demand balance. Demand stays relatively stable, as many of these products represent staples consumed for life. Although the harvest period may be spread over several months or even longer if international supplies are included, the supply is focused on one period of the year even though the market continues throughout the year. The market is, therefore, influenced by the perception of how plentiful the harvest has been, which may not play out in practice.

Meat

To some, the meat trade is part of agriculture, but when it comes to commodities, meat must be considered in a different way than grains and cereals. Once again, it pays to study farming and the factors that affect meat production before spending too much money trading in it. Meat includes various types of cattle, live hogs, and other animals.

The effect of the seasons on meat is a little more predictable than for crops. While crops may be destroyed by bad weather or weather may stop the harvest being taken, the effect on meat production is less. There is a knock-on effect in that the live animals may need to be fed with one of the crops in short supply, but overall, the production of the meat is not so sensitive. Seasons will also influence demand. There will be a need for more turkeys during Thanksgiving, and a hot summer may increase the desire for steaks to cook on the barbecue.

The other difference with meat is the time of presenting the animals to the market can be manipulated. Hungry animals represent pure overhead costs to the farmer once they are up to weight, but a glut can be avoided by keeping them for a month or two longer and, thus, getting a better price. Recent downturns in the farming economy during 2009 mean many smaller farmers have been forced to sell their herds for whatever they can get, which has depressed prices, and some have even been forced into bankruptcy. It remains to be seen what long-term effect this may have on the meat markets.

With the futures markets in meat, it is important the trader does not lose sight of the original purpose of futures and how this influences the costs. Farmers and processors will still be using the contracts to hedge their investment against uncertainties, and this will cause effects on the contract prices. The majority of trading, perhaps 85 percent, is for speculation, but this leaves 15 percent of traders affected by physical factors and who will take out contracts accordingly to protect their livelihood.

Metals

As a commodity, metals have been traded more frequently in recent years because of countries such as China and India experiencing rapid growth and industrialization, otherwise known as the emerging markets. China's economy has grown enormously, and with the wealth achieved by selling massively to the United States, Chinese citizens are poised to become more westernized in their tastes and consumption habits.

There are two classes of metals traded. One is the precious metal sector, principally recognized as gold and silver and including many other lesser-known materials, such as titanium and uranium. The other class of metals is the industrials, which include the metals that make up many things we buy. Examples of these are copper, heavily used for electrical wiring and components due to its excellent electrical conductivity, and steel, the basis of most manufacturing projects.

These two classes of metals are viewed differently by investors. The precious metal sector is traditionally one invested in during times of uncertainty in the markets and when high inflation is expected. It has benefited from the world economic crisis of 2008 and 2009, and gold investing has become popular and pushed the price beyond $1,000 per ounce for the first time.

Precious metals generally have a limited supply. The mines they are found in get depleted, and new exploration is required constantly to identify new reserves in the ground. Once seams are found, it can take several years to set up a mining operation and start meaningful production. As prices increase and techniques are improved, it becomes more cost effective to mine the less pure ores that may have been ignored previously, but the general supply picture is production is relatively fixed and not capable of responding quickly to changing demands. Thus, the price is mainly driven by the demand.

Sensitivity to demand is what has driven the price of gold up, and though a retracement in price may result from the overwhelming public interest in investing in gold causing the values to overshoot, it seems the underlying reasons for a steadily increasing price are sound. At the time of writing, in early 2010, there is a stock market recovery, which does not seem to be wholly supported by the underlying health of the economy, and there are enormous amounts of money entering the economy as part of the stimulus plan. Additional money in circulation fuels inflation, so if the cash injection materializes as money being spent, inflation in the long term will be the consequence. Any short-term market manipulation, such as suggested by some observers, will of necessity bow to fundamentals in due course.

Silver is in many ways a more interesting investment prospect than gold, despite its position as the "other precious metal." In contrast to the ways gold is used, silver is consumed, which may result in a significant shortage in the future. Most of the gold ever mined is still available, whether as jewelry, coinage, or gold ingots for investment, but this is not true of silver. Silver is used up incrementally, going into batteries, brazing material to join metals, electroplating, and photographic processes, and new uses are being discovered all the time. The amount of silver available in the world is reducing each year, despite current mining. As silver is mined largely as a byproduct of other metal production, it is not easy to increase the output. The U.S. Treasury now measures its silver reserves in millions rather than billions of ounces. The latest government figures show around seven million ounces in reserve. The peak amount was more than two billion ounces in 1959, about 300 times as much.

This shortage of silver means the market is much more volatile than that of gold, which means the trader must be more cautious when learning to trade in it. The commodities trading on the New York Commodities and Mercantile Exchange has promised to deliver, via futures contracts, more than twice the amount of silver that exists in the world today, and this is potentially a volatile situation that could easily result in dramatic economic events. For comparison, futures contracts in gold currently in place only promise about 2.5 percent of the current worldwide gold inventory.

The prices of industrial metals are influenced by a different set of circumstances. Because they make up consumer goods and depend on consumer spending, the industrial metals are subject to the current economic cycles and the health of the economy in general. When the economy is perceived to be shaky, investors run to the precious metals. When the economy is booming, industrial metals are in demand. The developing countries are also responsible for demand in the industrials, so even with a slow domestic economy, other forces can affect the prices.

In some ways, industrial metals can be easier to trade than precious metals. There are more obvious indicators of potential price movements with industrial metals, as they are directly needed and consumed in production. Precious metals are more dependent on investor sympathy, as few people really "need" to buy gold. Gold is bought because the investor wants a safe haven or because a trader thinks it will increase in value.

As an example of an industrial metal, copper has uses in many products and industries. It is often used for piping in smaller sizes such as used in housing, and aluminum has made little inroads into the electrical wiring market where copper is the natural choice. Copper is also used in high-tech electronics, such as printed circuit boards and electrical contacts. Due to its connection with construction, the housing market influences the price of copper, and a construction boom is sure to increase the demand. When the housing market turns downward, as it did in 2007, there is less need. Again, it is not as simple as determining the demand and assuming prices will inexorably rise if demand increases. If it were that obvious, many more traders would be millionaires.

However, assessing the market is important to determine the general trends and probabilities guiding your trading plan.

Shares

Stocks and shares represent investments in traded companies. The terms stocks and shares are often used interchangeably, though sometimes shares imply only one company, and stocks can refer to investments in several companies. The price of the shares reflects the market's perception of the future value of the company.

The price of the shares may be estimated in several ways. If the company pays dividends, the share value may be related to the expected ongoing income from them; when the company does not pay dividends, the calculation is going to consider the expected future value of the shares.

The shares issued by a company are equity shares in ownership of the company. If the company ceased trading, the shareholders could realize the value of the company's physical assets and good reputation in order to get something back. Although the value of all the shares issued is sometimes below the asset value, this gives another measure of a fair price.

Price will also be estimated with all sorts of analysis. The basic method of deciding on the long-term merits of a company is called fundamental analysis. This involves researching the basics, such as the profit and loss, operating costs, sales figures, range of products, and other factors. One metric frequently used is the price to earnings ratio, or the P/E ratio, which considers the price of the shares compared to the company's earnings. This can be compared with other companies in the same business to see whether the numbers are rational and in line with expectations.

Fundamental analysis considers the underlying values and seeks to determine how shares in a company deserve to be priced. There is another layer of complication to the price, however, as the market will not always fully reflect the values calculated. This side of the market is approached by considering technical analysis, which is concerned more with the day-to-day fluctuations in price.

Technical analysis considers the market sentiment to a particular company and does so by examination of a range of "indicators" produced from trading information. Learning from the way traders actually buy and sell the shares, technical analysts project the future short-term price movements and base their trading decisions on such information.

These techniques of valuing a company must be place in the context of understanding what a company does and its position in the marketplace and reading the news on the market sector. There is no one indicator or system that can always predict the best investment, but by a process of examining all available angles on the company and its performance, traders make their rational choices and select the stocks to buy.

Bonds

Bonds are often mentioned in the same breath as stocks but are actually different. They are a debt instrument, issued by a company or government to raise capital by borrowing money. Where stocks represent actual ownership of a company, for better or worse, bonds represent money lent to the company that must be repaid by a certain date and on which interest is paid, usually at regular intervals. Provided the company is sound, bonds retain their value in the long term and provide the investor with income. There is no such guarantee with stocks.

Treasury bonds, notes, and bills are issued by the U.S. government and are regarded as an extremely safe investment, though the interest paid is not high. Bonds are available for 30 years until maturity. Treasury notes are issued for periods of two, three, five, seven, and ten years, and Treasury bills, or T-bills, are issued for terms of less than a year. The 30-year bond was not issued for four years, from February 2002, but the government started selling them again in February 2006.

Bonds, as described, are considered safe, particularly in comparison to stocks. However, this does not mean they are always a constant value. If held to maturity, the price paid for the bond will be returned, but on the path to maturity, the values can change significantly. This is because of the interest rate of the bond and the prevailing market interest rate, so when the underlier of a derivative is a bond, it is regarded as a form of interest rate derivative.

In order to understand why a bond should vary in value — even when it has a certain face value — consider this example. Suppose you had a 10-year bond with a face value of $100, which was paying 6 percent interest every year. After five years, you needed the money, so you decided to sell the bond. Suppose again that the interest rate paid on bonds was now only 4 percent. The question is how much is the bond worth?

An investor with $100 could buy a new 5-year bond and get $4 interest for each of the five years plus the $100 back at the end, a total of $120. If the investor instead bought the bond from you, they would be much better off, getting $6 interest each year and the $100 in five years, for a total of $130.

Clearly if you only asked $100 for your bond, investors would be lining up at your door for the chance to make the additional income. If you asked for $110 for your bond, it would not be such a deal, as the investor would only get $20 profit after five years, just as he or she could if they only invested $100. The real value is somewhere between $100 and $110. There are calculations that can be done to arrive at the true value of the bond, but the principle is clear. Although they are a relatively secure place to invest, bonds do not have a static value.

Foreign currency

Trading on the foreign exchange market (forex) has become widely advertised and a realistic option for a few traders. It is a five-day, 24-hours–a-day market that offers excellent leverage for those on the winning side. Derivative contracts usually take place over a much longer time span than most forex traders are used to, but knowledge of the daily market moves can help give some background for your futures trading choices.

Many people first encounter foreign exchange when they vacation abroad, but the trading markets are different from the tourist exchanges you may have used. To be involved successfully with forex, the trader needs to keep up on international politics and the risks of different motivations of foreign governments. The FX market is so large it is almost impossible for there to be any significant manipulation by large investors, so in that way, it is a more equitable market for the small trader. Opposing this fact, which seems to allow the individual to trade on the same basis as the institutional trader, the governmental influences may prove to be less predictable than ordinary markets, so foreign currency trading carries with it some unique problems.

One of the governmental tools that impacts currency exchange is the setting of national interest rates by the central bank of each country — the Federal Reserve Bank in the United States.

Money naturally seeks the higher rates, increasing the demand for these currencies and changing the balance between different countries. For the novice trader who wants to pursue trading in currencies, the best advice is to restrict him or herself initially to just one or two others and thoroughly learn the influences and cycles of their values before taking on markets across the world.

When the underlier is a derivative

Derivatives of the underliers are what this book is about, but it is also possible for the underliers to be derivatives in their own right. As you have already learned, a derivative is something that derives its value from another thing, and that other thing can easily be a derivative itself.

The most common way this combination appears is with buying an option on a future. For instance, on the CME, it is possible to trade the S&P 500 Futures Option contract. The trader buys an option that gives them the right, but not the obligation, to buy an S&P 500 Futures contract at a certain price by a certain date. If the price is good, they can exercise the option and buy the futures at an advantageous price over the market rate; however, if not, the option can be allowed to expire worthless.

CASE STUDY: A TECHNICAL INNOVATOR

Dennis Hudson
Quantitative analyst and inventor
of Forward Looking Information
Radar (FLIR)
www.orangequant.com

Dennis Hudson is a quant trader of options. A quant is a quantitative analyst of financial information. He is the author of FLIR2 and other works, including Trainwreck, *whose June 2007 publication forecast in precise detail the coming crash. He honed his quant skills at General Electric in the late 1960s, forecasting particle size distributions in the*

manufacture of diamonds. He can be reached through his website:
www.orangequant.com.

Of all the derivative choices, I prefer the simplest plain vanilla stock option contracts, American-style. In this financial climate, I trade long only (buy only). I prefer these for the intrinsic leverage. Option contracts also enable me to indirectly trade in more expensive stocks, which often offer better liquidity and fewer surprises. By trading using the simplest methods, I avoid the problems that ensue during extreme volatility like what we have seen the last couple of years.

The thing that led me to derivatives was the money, the money, and the money. The intrinsic leverage was irresistible. As a quant, I was also attracted by the idea of needing to pinpoint moves across a narrow time period, something that is a big part of quantitative analysis. Also, decades ago and long before I started trading, I had a friend who did very well in options, and I never forgot it.

The current financial situation has affected my trading. To be very frank — and this was before I completed my current suite of algorithms, including h2o5 and synthetic trendlines — from March 6, 2009 through mid-June 2009, I took a terrible beating. My old algorithms kept saying the market could not sustain the climb, so I kept hitting it with puts. They were killing me. And that's what led me to develop a fresh set of approaches. Things have been better since then.

I think the excitement of derivatives for me is the leveraged potential, but also the fact I do not have to do as much research as when I was trading stocks only. Screening stocks had become a daily grind, but with options, I now only have to examine a few underlying issues and make my choices.

What do I dislike most about derivatives? It seems to me that beginning in March 2008 "someone" invented a new game. In simple terms, the new game was "Let's Make Puts and Calls Both Lose, No Matter What." It is not a fair game; that is, it is not a zero-sum game. Not that we should expect options to always be zero-sum, but it should be that way most of the time. Instead, the underlying stock moves in a certain direction — let's say up, favoring calls, one would expect, and crushing puts — but it moves so slowly that it eats up time premium and flattens volatility so both calls and puts get crushed. You could be right about direction but still lose. This makes a strong argument for watching historical volatility (intrinsic to the stock) and delta (change in option value relative to change in stock value) much more closely before entry. That works but can get tedious, so I finally sidestepped the issue with a custom indicator to yield inflections; arguably, that is incorporating intrinsic volatility, but at least I do not have to guess anymore at volatility shifts.

The personal qualities that help me in my chosen career include an inclination to caution, which is what helps me most, along with a sense of the need to stay organized in my thinking and calculations. The biggest success I have had in derivatives was the September/October 2008 crash of Hartford Financial Services (HIG). I kept laying on puts, taking profits, and laying them on again. Volatility kept dealing me aces.

The biggest challenge I have had to face is myself. I had a strong tendency to keep seeking the Holy Grail of algorithms — it is what quants do — but that can be a destructive tendency as well because you keep changing plans and not really building gains. No matter how great the algo is, there is a learning curve for discovering its quirks. I had to stop jumping around and use what works.

If I was giving advice to someone who wanted to begin trading in derivatives, first of all, I would say find what works for you and stick to it. Second, keep your trade sizes modest — that is how I got away with so much experimenting for so many years.

Chapter 8

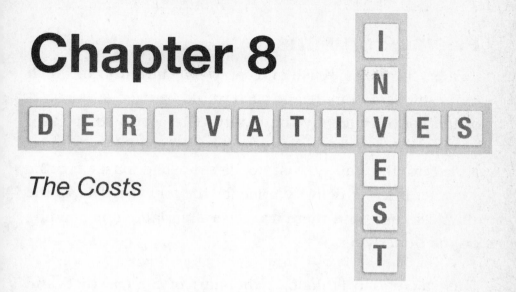

DERIVATIVES

The Costs

Chapter 3 introduced one way to value derivatives using a cash-and-carry method and the concept that the price of a forward or futures contract is initially neutral to both parties. If it is not, then one party would be unwilling to enter into the contract. What happens after the contract has been taken out is what makes the profit or loss for the participants in the market.

Options are slightly different in that the option buyer is spending money on a gamble that the market will move in his or her favor and buying the privilege of only going through with the contract if it is profitable. In effect, the premium is like an insurance against a losing commitment. Many of the same principles, such as the time value of money, apply to this market too.

Pricing Forwards

Earlier, the idea of "cash and carry" was introduced, which in its simplest form means cash would be used at the start of the contract to buy the equity. The cost of that cash, or cost of carry — typically interest charges — would be added to the equity cost to give a solid basis for the contract price or delivery price for the forward. This is the simplest case, and there are several variations depending on the underlying.

This calculation is done at the start of the contract, and fortunes are made or lost by what happens to the price of the underlying subsequently. However, the contract price must be neutral to both parties at the outset.

The long party, who will be buying the equities at the agreed delivery price in the future, will be speculating the equities increase in value beyond that price. The short party, who will need to provide the equities in the future, could just "cash and carry" them, but there might be little point in doing this. If speculating for a profit, the short party would be hoping the equity price reduced before the delivery date, so they could be bought cheaper later and a profit made.

This simple way of pricing a forward can be expressed as an equation:

Delivery price = spot price + carry cost

The delivery price, or contract price, is easy to understand and is fixed once the contract is in place. The spot price, or market price, is likely to fluctuate, which may provide the profit for either party. In the equation, the spot price is the price of the commodity at the time the contract is taken out. The carry cost may have several components and will also depend on what the underlying commodity is.

In its most basic form, the carry cost is the interest charged for borrowing cash and buying the underlying on the day the contract is agreed. Later on, we will consider other costs of carry, but for now, we will focus on the interest cost. This cost is often based on the LIBOR, as this is a published and readily available rate of interest. Another standard interest rate is the prime rate, which is the rate at which a bank will lend to its best customers.

The essence of a calculation is the interest rate should be at a risk-free or commonly available level. Other interest rates could be used, but if they involve an element of risk, they would not give the required neutral pricing to the forward contract.

If the underlying are shares, there is the possibility a dividend will be issued while they are held by the short party, and this would modify the carry cost. It would benefit the short party, and therefore, the total carry cost would be reduced. To the extent the issuing of the dividend can be predicted, it would be included when determining the delivery price for the forward contract. Large companies try to maintain or slightly increase the level of dividend they issue, so often the value can be reasonably foreseen.

The cost of carry can include many other factors depending on the nature of the underlier. For instance, there may be a cost for storage if the underlier is considered bought when the contract is taken out. Often, this would apply to commodity underliers, such as oil. Depending on the length of contract, some perishable commodities may not be suitable for storage, which introduces a further complication in the equation. For those that can be stored, the contract price calculation can be made and the cost of storage included.

Quite often oil presents a special case in which the spot price is actually higher than the forward delivery price. This effectively suggests a negative carry cost. One reason for this may be that large consumers routinely pay a premium to buy oil in the spot market in order to ensure they have sufficient quantities to maintain their supplies.

The foregoing ways of considering a fair price for a forward contract should not be taken to imply the provider, or short party, in the contract will actually purchase the underlying when agreeing to the contract. As stated above, there would be little point in doing this. Unless arbitrage opportunities exist, it would involve the short party in organizing, borrowing, purchasing, and possible storing with no prospect of profit. However, considering this could be done provides a sound basis from which to determine a fair value for the contract.

In practice, this provides only an approximation of the contract value. Other factors enter into the equation, such as transaction charges for buying shares, and storage charges may vary between suppliers depending on aspects such as whether the short party has an empty warehouse available. The arbitrage principle that drives the forward delivery price toward the calculated fair value is easy to understand. If the forward contract is priced higher, indeed, the short party could cash and carry and make a profit. If the forward contract price is below the fair value, then traders would go long on the forward contract and short the shares, which would allow them to buy the shares at a lower price on the delivery day to close the short position and make a profit.

Forex forwards are a special case of cash and carry, as they involve the interest rates in both the currencies. If the interest rates are not the same, the forward will be priced to take the difference into account. Depending on which currency has the higher interest rate, the forward may be priced above or below the current spot rate. For the cash and carry calculation, if the short party buys the currency when the contract is agreed and can receive a higher interest rate in the foreign currency than he or she is paying for the borrowed money that bought it, he or she is making a net amount of money from holding the currency.

Again, this simplification allows the speculator to understand the approximate value of the forward contract. In practice, there are factors such as the spread between the buying and selling spot prices for the currency and the difference between the interest rate charged when borrowing and paid when investing. Nevertheless, the same principle applies if the price drifts too far from the calculated fair value. If there is an arbitrage opportunity greater than these adjustments, then traders will spot it, and their actions will serve to close the gap between the quoted price and the fair value.

Pricing Futures

Having covered the pricing of forward contracts, it would be easy to think futures contracts work in exactly the same way, as the principal of agreeing on a price for a sale at a future date is identical. This does apply to a certain extent, but there are differences because of the way futures contracts are traded. It is conventional to apply the cash and carry method to determine a starting point for the fair value, but while a forward contract is only settled at the expiration, futures contracts are valued every day.

This means the value of a futures contract is the difference between today's and yesterday's price. All other changes in price have already been settled up into the account at the end of yesterday's trading.

This system of a margin account means there is a high degree of protection against default. As the exchange is responsible for the satisfaction of each contract, the system protects the exchange from serious losses. The interesting point with futures is the contract price does not move in concert with the spot price of the underlying. Changes in price occur not only because of theoretical changes in carry costs but also because of speculative trading. This is a function of the system, set up with standardized contracts to allow liquidity in the market and, therefore, encourages active trading and speculation.

Bear in mind that as the delivery date approaches, the futures contract gets closer to the spot price. On the delivery date, the difference between the futures contract price and the stock price is zero.

Pricing CFDs

As mentioned, the advantage of CFDs over normal trading is the leverage permitted. This is an idea shared with other derivatives. The actual leverage available will depend on the trader's relationship with his or her broker and is typically about ten to one. Thus, a 10-percent deposit can control a position.

Unlike futures or options, the CFD trader never has ownership of any shares and never has any rights to own shares. This is important for the UK market because it is the reason a trader can avoid stamp duty. The UK government views CFDs as a form of betting rather than investing, which frees the trader from some tax liabilities.

Your broker, however, may invest in the shares to hedge his or her position. Most equity CFD providers will do this to minimize their risk. As result of this hedging, your broker is not exposed to losses and does not have to guess the market. If you make a profit, then your broker makes the same from his or her shareholding and has no financial exposure.

Your broker may charge a commission or, in some cases, make a profit by the spreads between the bid and ask prices. Commission may be anything up to a quarter percent of the contract value or may be a fixed commission. In the latter case, you may find the spread between the bid and ask prices is larger, so be sure to shop around for an economical broker. Commission is usually charged for buying the CFD and selling it, so you may pay around a half percent total.

The other cost of trading CFDs, as mentioned above, is an interest charge for trading on margin. Often, this interest rate is 6 to 8 percent per year or roughly 0.02 percent per day. If you buy and sell a CFD on the same day, you do not incur any interest charges. As with trading futures, if there is a dividend due while you have a contract open, you will have an adjustment on your account. If you are long in the CFD, you will receive a dividend payment, and if you are short, you will incur a debit to your account in the amount of the declared dividend.

If you are trading index CFDs instead of trading CFDs on individual shares, you will usually find no commission is charged. Instead, the broker's profit for the trade will come from the spread between the bid and ask prices, which would be in the region of three to six points. An alternative method involves basing the CFD price on the futures market adjusted to the fair value. As index CFDs are available on many of the world markets, note that the price is always quoted in the base currency of the index, regardless of where you are trading.

Pricing Options

Pricing options is more difficult than pricing futures or forwards as it involves a transaction that may not happen, depending on the price movements. It is hard to decide on a value for a contract when the profit or loss does not vary smoothly, as with futures, and is uncertain. The fact that the buyer of an option only takes it up if it is profitable means, in theory, the odds of profitability are built into the premium paid, but as the rewards are variable, there is no easy solution as in the cash and carry method.

First, consider the extremes. A call option allows purchase of the shares at the option price, regardless of where the shares are trading on the expiration date. Without waiting for the expiration, you could buy the shares at the current market price and have them at the expiration date regardless of their value then. Therefore, any call option can be worth no more than the actual stock price; if it were, you would be better off buying the shares now rather than the option. Similarly, a put option cannot cost more than taking a short position in the stock.

These are the extreme positions, but it is possible to be much more precise when pricing individual options. One of the most well-known ways of determining a fair price for European options is known as the Black-Scholes model.

Myron Scholes and Robert Merton, who also worked on the model, received the Nobel Prize for it in 1997, more than 20 years after their initial work.

The premium paid for an option consists of two parts. One part is called the intrinsic value, always zero or above, and the other part is the time value. The intrinsic value must always be above zero because the holder of the option is never obliged to exercise it, which allows traders to avoid incurring negative values. The time value is an amount that represents the chance the option will be in the money on expiration. The longer the option has to run, other things being equal, the greater the time value, as it represents the chance the price will change to make the option in the money or increase the amount by which it is in the money.

It is possible to delve in much greater depth into option pricing using calculus, but on the assumption most readers do not have mathematics degrees, the essential concepts necessary to trading options will be discussed in layman's terms.

Any discussion of option pricing must be based on probabilities. The outcome is, obviously, unknown, so the value is based on the range of possible future values of the option and the probabilities of each occurring. Every model developed to derive a fair option premium must be based on this concept.

Concept of expected payoff

The start to valuing an option is to consider the expected payoff. This is an idea used in economics that helps decide whether to make a risky investment or take a chance on a bet. In essence, you need to consider all possible payoffs from the bet or investment and multiply or weight each according to how likely they are to happen.

For example, say an investor was asked to put $10,000 into a start-up business. By some means (the details are not needed to understand the example), the investor determines that with a 25-percent probability his or her money may be doubled to $20,000, with a 40-percent probability the investment will be worth $15,000, and with a 35-percent probability he or she will lose all his or her money. The question is, does this represent a worthwhile opportunity?

The way to find this out is to calculate the expected payoff from the deal:

**The expected payoff =
($20,000 x 25%) + ($15,000 x 40%) + ($0 x 35%) =
$11,000**

As the expected payoff is $11,000 and the investor is only being asked for $10,000, this deal can be considered a good one. On average, the investor will come out ahead. Whether the investor takes part in the deal depends on his or her risk tolerance, as over one third of the time he or she will lose all of the investment. This does not change the fact it works out to be a profitable deal, on balance.

As explained, this is a simple concept, though putting values on probabilities can be difficult. Provided there is confidence in the numbers, this is a powerful method for determining the value of a deal with different possible outcomes and consequently leads to a method of option pricing.

An option can lead to several different outcomes, each of which has its own probability of occurring. Therefore, the value of an option contract must be the expected payoff, as this will be the fair amount to pay the option writer. If it was any less, no one would want to write the option, as they would be bound to lose over time. If the option contract was priced higher than the expected payoff, any knowledgeable trader would not want to buy the option. The difficulty, and the mathematics, is in determining a real value for the expected payoff.

It is worth noting the option buyer always has a positive expected payoff. As the option will not be exercised if the value is negative, the outcomes that count will be zero or a positive number. Whether the option is profitable depends on the premium charged, which in a perfect model would exactly equal the expected payoff.

Black-Scholes model

As mentioned earlier in this chapter, the Black-Scholes model is one of many devised to more closely estimate the fair price of an option and is arguably the most famous model. In its basic form, it applies to European-style options, the options only exercised on the expiration date and not at any time before. The option value is the expected payoff at the expiration date, with the value discounted back to the day the option was purchased. This gives the theoretical amount that should be paid for the option contract.

There are only five factors that have to be put into this model to determine the option price. The first is the current spot price for the underlying shares. The strike or exercise price in the option contract is the second factor. The third input is the amount of time left until the expiry date or exercise date of the option. These three inputs are absolutely determinable, so this is not where the difficulty in valuation lies.

The other two factors are subject to some uncertainty. The important fourth factor is a measure of the volatility in the price of the stock, and this merits some further discussion. The fifth factor is the interest rate, or cost of carry, which does not have such a great effect but can still vary the outcome.

Without quoting the actual Black-Scholes equation here, the direction in which each of these factors will affect the option pricing is still evident. If the stock price increases, the call option will be more expensive and a put option will be cheaper. The call option is more likely to be in the money or further into the money for a larger profit if the stock price is already higher, and vice versa for a put. In a similar way, if the strike price is lower and the call option is more valuable, the option price will be more expensive. If the strike price is higher, the put option will be more expensive.

The time left until expiration has the effect of increasing the values of the call and put options. This is because there is more opportunity for the price to change. If there is a year to expiry, there is much more chance the price of a share can change substantially than if there is only one day left. As stated earlier, the longer the option has to run, the greater the time value will be.

When the volatility is greater, call options and put options will be more expensive. The argument is the same as for the time to expiration: With greater volatility, as with a longer time, there is more chance that the option will expire in the money.

Finally, an increase in interest rate or cost of carry will increase the value of a call option but will reduce the value of a put. This relates to the opportunity cost of having money to invest. If you buy a call option instead of buying the shares today, you will have most of your money to put into an interest-bearing account; therefore, a higher interest rate means the call option must be more expensive because you will be earning more interest. If your choice is between buying a put option and selling the shares, buying the put option means you do not have the money to invest, so a higher interest rate causes a greater opportunity cost and, therefore, a cheaper option.

Back now to volatility, as this is perhaps the hardest variable to pin down. Understanding volatility is the key to understanding option pricing. The statistical measure of volatility is called the standard deviation of a value. This term comes from probability theory, which examines the expected values of a variable. The distribution of values can be shown graphically as what is classically called a bell curve, as it forms the shape of a bell. The X-axis — the horizontal one — represents the possible values. The Y-axis is the number of occurrences. The actual value of the standard deviation from the mean is what covers 68 percent of the occurrences. The majority of the values are centered around the middle of the bell pattern where the bell is highest, and the volatility is shown by how wide the bell is.

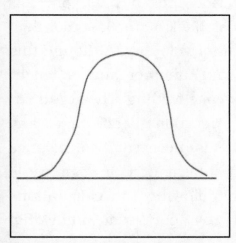 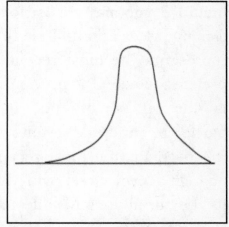

Figure 1: Bell Curve High Standard Deviation

Figure 2: Bell Curve Low Standard Deviation

As volatility is key to option pricing, there have been a number of studies into how best to determine the volatility of the security at any particular time. You will appreciate that a security's volatility can change over time. For example, the markets may be more turbulent this year than last, but the initial starting point for the volatility measurement is in looking at the past price behavior.

The starting point for determining volatility is usually the historical volatility the share has exhibited in the past. This is a simple statistical calculation for a computer to make, and the standard deviation is worked out on the percentage changes in price over a historical period. The standard deviation is expressed as a percentage; if it was expressed in dollar terms, it would make comparison between different value shares difficult.

A major choice that needs to be made in order to calculate historical volatility is the period looked back on. For instance, you may choose to look back on the last month of closing prices and analyze that for volatility. Although this represents the most recent data, another analyst might prefer to look on the previous year's trading. The argument is this will smooth out disproportionate effects of any particular unusual events. It is necessary to balance the need for the most recent information, if volatility is changing over time, with not allowing the calculations to be dramatically affected by particular individual circumstances.

Historical volatility is a good starting point for pricing an option as the information is readily available and the calculation is straightforward given modest computing power. The two problems with historical volatility are:

1. The selection of an appropriate length of time. There is no one correct answer to this, as it depends on the price behavior of the stock.

2. The fact that historical volatility can only reflect what has happened in the past, and the true value required is what will happen in the future over the life of the option. There is obviously no way to know this.

To some extent, it is possible to rely on and appropriately modify the historical volatility. If a review of the history of the company shows its trading as relatively unchanged in the past two years, the historical volatility is more likely to be close to the future volatility. If the history of the company shows a management buyout or other events that cause instability in the price, it may be possible to take a view the historical volatility is higher than would be expected in the future. A consequence of this is the company may be in an industry where a takeover is likely in the future, and volatility can increase.

There is an alternative approach to determining volatility that reflects the markets opinion of the security. This is called "implied volatility." As options are freely available and the premiums are published, it is possible to work the model backward to see what value the markets are placing on the volatility. Remember with the Black-Scholes model, the first three factors are known, and the interest rate or cost of carry can be reasonably estimated. It is then a simple mathematical exercise to determine what volatility the market is expecting by the option prices exhibited.

As much as this may seem a curious way to approach the problem of determining volatility, implied volatility is widely used by institutional investors, risk managers, and dealers to determine values and form an opinion of overpriced options. With an efficient market assumed, implied volatility will include the knowledge and experience of all the market participants based on currently available information.

Another way in which implied volatility can be used is by the trader seeking pricing on various options from the broker and working out the assumed volatilities associated with those prices. If the trader finds one of the option choices has an implied volatility less than he or she would expect from independent observation, the option becomes a good candidate for trading because the expected payoff will be more than the premium charged.

You may be wondering about the significance of calculating implied volatility to determine an option price when it is that very option price you are using to find the volatility. On the face of it, this is a circular argument. The key to realizing its usefulness is to note there are many options available for any individual stock. Options are available with different strike prices, the agreed contract price, and by playing around with the equations, you will find some options are relatively mispriced.

As with all things, real life is not quite as straightforward as determining one volatility for a particular stock. It is likely you will find different volatilities for different strike prices, and the reasons are not always clear. Sometimes it may be a trader preference, and other times, it may be due to less obvious factors. Some traders blame the Black-Scholes model, and this has resulted in the formulation of different models that have names like stochastic volatility and jump diffusion and attempt to refine the pricing calculation.

You might also expect the implied volatility to be consistent for any particular strike price over a range of expiry dates. Again, this would probably not be the case. All of this means analysts continue to work to improve on Black-Scholes by seeking more refined methods to identify anomalies in pricing that can result in profit.

The Greeks

In any detailed discussion of options amongst traders, the conversation will inevitably turn to "the Greeks." In summary, the Greeks measure the sensitivity of the option value to the inputs in the pricing model. They describe in numbers how much the option premium will vary as the inputs vary. Such knowledge is useful when you are trying to manage risk in your trading.

There are five Greeks commonly used to describe the model sensitivities. They are called Greeks because they are represented by five letters from the Greek alphabet: delta (δ), gamma (γ), theta (φ), kappa (κ), and rho (ρ). Sometimes kappa is called vega, but this is not a Greek letter. In calculus, these values would be called derivatives in the pricing model, as they measure the rate of change. This is not to be confused with the financial term derivative.

Starting first with delta, this term defines the way the option premium varies with a change in value of the underlying. Usually, when exploring these factors it is assumed the other inputs to the model are held constant. Delta is always positive, which means the value of the call option increases as the underlying price increases.

As a rule, delta is about 0.5 when an option is at the money. This means a small change in share price will change the option price about half as much. This makes some intuitive sense, as there is a 50-percent chance of the price going up or down and varying the option outcome.

When an option is out of the money, delta will be less and will tend toward zero if the option is a long way out of the money. As the option is unlikely to be exercised, variations in the price of the underlying do not affect the option premium by much.

In summary, delta can vary between zero and one. The value depends on how the strike price compares with the current or spot price. The value is just an approximation and should not be used to cover large changes in spot price, as the delta would need to vary over a range. This effect is sometimes called positive gamma, which brings us to the second Greek.

Gamma adds a degree of complication to delta. Gamma is a measure of the change expected in delta for a small change in the stock price. It provides a value for the sensitivity of delta, so in mathematical terms, it is called a second-order value. It quantifies a change in a change.

Considering the way delta performs, it is possible to understand the general form of gamma. When the option is out of the money, delta is small and does not change much. The option price will not change much with changes in the spot price. This means gamma is also small.

Conversely, when the option is deeply into the money, delta is nearly one because any change in stock price is directly reflected on the profit from the option. In this case, a call option is similar to having a long position in the share, and it does not change much, so gamma is small.

When an option is at the money, delta will change in value to the greatest extent as the stock price changes. Accordingly, gamma is at its highest value. As it is a modifier of delta, which itself only varies between zero and one in the whole range of spot prices, even at its maximum, gamma is still a small value, typically around 0.01.

Next of the Greeks is theta, a variable that defines the change in value of an option for any given change in time to the expiration date. Again, this is considered in isolation, with all other inputs to the model remaining constant. As options tend to go down in value as the expiration approaches, theta is normally negative for a long option, regardless of whether it is a call or a put option.

Theta is normally measured as cents per day loss in value, but note that theta is not a constant and depends on how far the option is from expiration. When it gets to the last few days, theta increases rapidly. One day's difference in the option price when there is still a month to run is much less than a day's difference when the option has two days until its expiration date.

The next Greek is kappa, or vega as it is commonly called, which measures the change in the value of the option for a given change in volatility. Vega is a positive value for a call option and a put option, which is easy to deduce from the knowledge that an option premium increases with greater volatility. In contrast to the previous Greeks, there is almost a linear relationship between the option value and the volatility, so for every percent increase in volatility, there will be an equal increase in option pricing. Vega is normally quoted as a number for each 1 percent volatility change.

The final Greek is rho, which measures the change in value of an option for a change in interest rate, again with all other factors being kept constant. For a call option, rho will be positive, which means the option price will increase as the cost of borrowing goes up. This is seen to be true because the buyer of an option could invest the money required to buy the shares at the strike price until the expiry date. Holding the option rather than the shares would give the trader income, reflected in the price of the option. By the same logic, with higher interest rates, the benefit is greater and the option is more expensive.

For a put option, rho would be negative. This also makes sense if you think about it from the point of view of the option writer; the writer must buy the shares if the option is exercised. To hedge against a fall in the value of the shares, the writer could choose to take a short position in them and invest the proceeds until expiration. The short position means he or she would be compensated if the share value fell. If the interest rate were to rise, there will be more money paid in interest by the deposit, and therefore, the writer could charge less as a premium for the put option.

Pricing Swaps

Now on to the question of pricing swaps. As previously mentioned, swaps involve exchanging future payments, typically a fixed-rate interest for a floating-rate interest. As such, swaps can be considered a series of future payments or cash flows, and there is a standard accounting way to discount future cash flows back to the present. All that has to happen is each payment is discounted back to the present, and the payments are totaled.

Interest rates are involved in the price of the underlying and in working out the discounts. Usually, these rates are different. Interest rates will also vary depending on the length of time money is borrowed or deposited, as you can easily see when you consider the different rates offered by the U.S. Treasury on their notes, bills, and bonds that have different maturity dates. This is usually taken care of by plotting what is called a "yield curve," a chart of percentage rates against length of time. The interest rates usually increase the longer the money is invested.

The actual calculation is laborious and is best carried out by a computer program rather than manually. The present day value of the floating payments must be computed for each. This requires interpreting the interest rate applicable from the yield curve and counting the number of days until the payment is due. Applying the interest, the value of the payment in the future is calculated, and the discount rate is applied to this sum to determine a present value of that payment.

This must be done for each of the floating rate payments, which is why the use of a computer program is advised. Once you have a list of present values for all the payments to be made, this can be summed to a grand total, the present cost of the floating rate portion of swap.

Given that the swap should start with no bias on either side, the second part of the calculation is to determine the fixed rate equivalent to the present value of the floating rate leg. The payments for the fixed rates may not be on the same schedule as the floating rate payments, which would introduce further complication. Before computers were used, this would entail working through a calculation several times using different interest rates until the present value matched that of a floating leg of the swap. Now it can be calculated directly.

Note the value does not have to be exactly the same. If one party is contracting the interest rate swap for the benefit of another, it may be he or she would charge for the service. Instead of making a single upfront charge of perhaps $20,000, he or she could recover a fee by purposely mismatching the present values of the two legs of the contract. In this way, he or she may even achieve a greater fee because of the convenience to the other party.

Trading Costs

In a traditional stock market transaction, you would expect the broker to charge a commission on each deal. You pay the commission whenever you buy or sell any shares. Discount brokers may charge $10 or less, full-service brokers much more, and some charge as a percentage of the share price, with a minimum cost.

There are a variety of ways the broker or dealer in a derivative contract can be paid for his or her time and effort. They have been previously mentioned in the individual sections. When you set up an account to trade in futures, options, or other derivatives, the dealer will give disclosure of the methods practiced, and it is your responsibility to make sure you understand them.

In many cases, there is a difference between the bid and the ask price quoted. This difference is called the spread and constitutes the broker's profit. It is usually not large, but with the quantities of contracts traded, the spread can amount to a reasonable profit. The difference between the bid and ask means you must have a certain minimum price move in your direction to break even. If you were to buy and sell again straight away, you would automatically lose money.

Another trading cost built into many of the derivative forms arises from the margining system used. This system is the key to multiplying the use of your money, which gives you leverage to control and profit from a greater value of assets or commodities than you could otherwise afford. When you open a position, your broker requires an initial margin that is a fraction of the total cost.

Each day, the positions you hold will be marked-to-market so the profits or losses are added to or deducted from your account. This can result in a margin call, which means your account is restored to the minimum level required by the broker or the exchange for you to continue to hold the position. If you are an active trader, you must always be able to put your hands on such additional money as is required; otherwise, you may find your position is closed out for you before it turns into profit.

The effect of the margin system is your trading profits and losses are realized every day in marked contrast to what you may have been used to trading stocks and shares. With stocks, a rising price is only a paper profit until you sell them; a falling price is not a loss until you close out the position, which may explain the trader's unfortunate reticence to cut his or her losses.

The margin call is not a profit to the broker or clearinghouse. There are two sides to each contract, and if you are long on shares that are falling in value and must pay a margin call, there is another trader who is in a short position and will receive the benefit of additional funds in his or her account. However, it is undoubtedly a trading cost that must be borne in mind and met when necessary.

Much of the time, trading on margin incurs further trading costs. The simple explanation for this is you are effectively borrowing the remainder of the value of the underlying over and above your initial margin, and borrowing money costs money in the form of interest. Again, this depends on which derivatives you trade and who you trade them with, and your broker or dealer should give you full details. In some instances, such as going short with a CFD, you may find your account is credited interest, but it will be at a far lower rate than you are charged when borrowing.

In addition to the costs you incur by the actual process of trading, there are many other costs you need to be aware of and include when planning to make a business of trading. Also, be aware that unless you approach trading as a business, you are unlikely to make a consistent income.

Your trading may include the setting up of a separate area to constitute an office, complete with a high-speed Internet connection and several monitors, which involves capital costs. The costs become much higher when you start to figure in the recurring subscriptions for high-speed data feeds, software, cable television, and other things you will find necessary, if not essential, to give yourself the tools you need for your new business.

If you talk to any successful trader, you will find they are committed to continuing self-improvement. Most make a point of attending seminars and taking courses, but at a minimum, they read about trading, in books and magazines. Some have even admitted when they stopped communicating, their trading began to suffer. You may have not given the topic much thought, but seriously consider committing a certain annual amount or proportion of your earnings into a continuing education fund so you can plan and take care of this expenditure.

Chapter 9

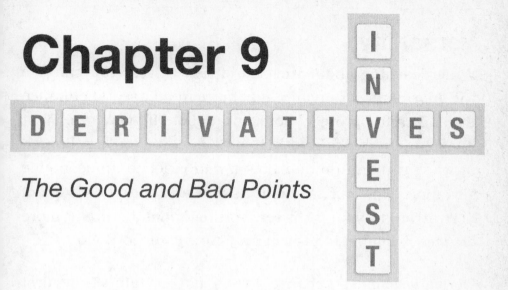

DERIVATIVES

The Good and Bad Points

Derivatives can be regarded as evil concoctions, as they were painted by the media when the financial crisis erupted, or they can be thought of as an efficient means to achieve specific financial objectives. They are neither. They are only tools used to achieve various ends, and what the outcome is depends on the way they are used.

With the help of this book, you will understand what you are getting into. Derivatives are powerful and must be used responsibly; otherwise, you can quickly get into trouble, and as the financial crisis has proven, being a financial professional does not protect you from the consequences of unsound investment. With that said, the following summarizes the pros and cons of using derivatives in your portfolio.

Versatility

While learning about the use of derivatives, you can see the enormous variety of ways they can be used to enhance trading and protect your portfolio. If you are just investing in stocks and bonds, it is clear you are limited in what you can do and how it can react to an economic situation. However, as soon as you add the knowledge of derivatives to your skill set, you also include many more choices available to protect and grow your portfolio.

Derivatives exist because life is not certain. They first existed to hedge costs for businesses, but because of their adaptability, many other people have discovered new uses for them and started making inordinate profits. Any discussion of derivatives inevitably involves risk, and used in a cautious way, they can moderate or eliminate risk to your portfolio.

You have seen from the initial chapters the tremendous variety of derivatives available. If it could be thought of, it has been invented. Knowledge of derivatives takes away the unreasonable fear and shows the ways in which they can benefit financial well-being.

In addition to the ways in which derivatives help a personal account, you have also learned to appreciate how derivatives help ordinary people go about their business. A farmer can plant with confidence having locked in a price for his or her crop. A business can expand, confident that its interest charges are contained because of an interest rate swap. Financial markets could not operate today without some element of the derivatives available, and pension funds can protect investor money even during financial downturns.

Powerful

Of course, one of the common threads and most attractive features of derivatives is the element of leverage available because they multiply the performance of your money. This came to the public's attention when they saw the outstanding performances of hedge funds, some of which used derivatives extensively.

Because of the way they are set up, hedge funds are not constrained to the extent mutual funds and regular bank accounts are. They are at liberty to take whatever financial positions they feel are in the best interest of investors. Largely, hedge funds are outside the regulation of the SEC because they are only open to "sophisticated investors," people with extensive resources or a major income. The SEC apparently considers such investors to be better able to protect their finances by reviewing exactly what the hedge fund manager is doing. Unfortunately, this means many people with ordinary resources and incomes have felt left out from the tremendous profits hedge funds often report, as they are not allowed to make such investments.

However, this exclusivity did encourage ordinary investors to explore the different types of financial instruments available, and as a consequence, there has been a great increase in interest in derivatives. It is now possible for an investor with modest means to avail him or herself of many of the derivatives to which hedge funds had laid claim, and the multiplying power of leverage has become much more widely used.

CASE STUDY: THRILLED BY THE PSYCHOLOGY

Stu Whisson
Lead trader trainer
Technical Analysis Training
www.insightsupport.com
stu@insightsupport.com

*Stu Whisson is the lead trader trainer at **www.insightsupport.com**, one of Europe's leading online trader training establishments, specializing in technical analysis. The website was set up by Whisson in 2003 and has since become a huge success. They have trained many successful traders, new and old, from all over the world. Visit the site today to gain access to renowned free online training courses and events.*

The sorts of derivatives I trade are mostly financial spread bets, which are predominantly a UK-specific (though becoming increasingly more popular in other countries), highly geared product — a contrary bet against that of the spread betting company and akin to futures in terms of gearing and price.

If you ask anyone who trades in financial spread bets, he or she will say the main reason for trading them is they are 100 percent tax-free. Being that they are classed as a bet, rather than essentially a trade, means in UK law the trade is void of any windfall taxes or other forms of tax. The other reasons for preferring these trades are financial spread bets are highly geared and do follow the market action very closely.

I originally started in the late '80s trading stocks — like many general consumers. Margaret Thatcher was privatizing many of the utilities, and they were being sold to the general public. It was from this that I became interested in the market and the psychology that drives the markets. I discovered financial spread betting after wanting to be involved in the futures market but not having the deep pockets required and certainly, at that point, out of the realm of possibility for someone in his late teens.

Like many traders, I believe I have become more cautious because of some large losses in the recent past. I do not believe there were many traders who were *not* financially bruised by the effects of the crash.

Few traders openly talk about loss, but essentially it is all a part of the same game, and you have to be as open about loss as you are with your gains. I say I am more cautious, but in many respects, it has stopped me from overtrading.

Apart from the obvious rewards, the thing that excites me most about derivatives is I like the fact that everyone, regardless of his or her account size, is essentially in the same position. We are all trying to second-guess one another. The whole psychology of this wonderful game is the thrill for me. I do not like the fact that so many get tied up with gains, though I can see why they do. After all, profit is what drives what we do; otherwise, no one would trade. However, I feel it is important to understand once you stop focusing on the profit and start enjoying the act of trading, not only do you take pleasure in the ride more, but a rather nice off-shoot of this attitude is you subsequently become more relaxed as a trader, and from experience, this has lead to greater profits. This is part of what I teach in my training of students interested in trading.

Regarding dislikes, I could go on about the possible losses, but then, as I have mentioned previously, this is all part of the wonderful world of trading. I do not really dislike anything about derivatives; they are what they are. You cannot have everything all one way, and despite the fact they can be quite challenging and bloody infuriating at times, the reward easily enables you to forget the subsequent frustrations that can arise.

For personal qualities, I feel a sense of detachment is all-important in trading — in any trading. When I first started trading, I would overly worry about each trade I made. I soon realized this was not helping me at all. Therefore, I have a massive sense of complete emotional detachment from all my trades. I am neither overly anal about my trading decisions nor too lax. It is a case of analyzing the market, making a decision, trading, and moving on. Once the decision is made, I do not stress about whether it was the right choice or not.

What was my biggest success? That is for me to know. I feel it impolite to talk of one's successes. It is an ugly form of gloating. Needless to say, I have had massive successes and, not so long ago, rather spectacular losses. I accept both with open arms and enjoy the ride along the way.

The biggest challenge I have had to face is always a personal one with trading. Going back to what I was saying about my personal qualities, I found I worried about my trades too much. This does not mean to say now I am a maverick and forget them completely. I do, of course, manage the trades and adjust them accordingly. As soon as the trade has been placed, I only concentrate on managing that trade accordingly. It took me a long time to get to this mind-set. As soon as I adopted it and made it part of who I am as a trader, my successes quickly took over my failures.

If someone wanted to follow in my footsteps, I would advise him or her not to follow in my footsteps but to learn from him or herself. Trading will show you emotional weakness in yourself. Therefore, only trade when you are emotionally together and willing to see your initial losses as a means of learning the ropes. Seek a good mentor, whether me or someone else. Someone you feel you can relate to, who is prepared to give you time and help you break down the emotional issues with trading. If someone were to tell me years ago the biggest battle with trading was myself, I would have laughed in his or her face. Now, having done this for more than 20 years, I can see how you approach trading has everything to do with your success. Get that part right and learn the technical analysis inside and out.

Hedging

A principal use of derivatives is to manage risk or hedge against a bad outcome. After all, this is principally why they were developed in the first place and why other forms have been developed during the years.

When discussing risk in this context, it is exclusively financial risk. Financial risk is the chance there may be some loss caused by uncertainty in the markets. Derivatives were invented to manage this risk and avoid potentially catastrophic events.

In essence, hedging involves recognizing where there is financial risk, quantifying it, and taking on a new position in a financial instrument that counters the possible losses. If there is a loss in the original security, then the new position should have a corresponding gain. You no longer need to worry if the original security is going to go down in value. If the worst does not happen, the hedge position may lose money, but this should be compensated by the original security increasing in value.

Hedging with derivatives employs leverage. In essence, this means managing risk with derivatives costs far less than it would otherwise. This is the advantage of knowing about and using derivatives for hedging. Most commonly, derivatives will be used to hedge against a risk or exposure to financial loss in a nonderivative financial security. Hedging can also be employed to protect a speculative position in derivatives, which is an important use, as missteps with speculation when employing leverage are potentially disastrous.

When selecting a derivative to use to hedge your position, bear in mind you want to have an exposure that is the opposite of the thing you are trying to hedge. For instance, if you own stock or are long on stock and you think the price may decline, you may hedge against this using futures or options. If you are long on stock, you would use a short position in a futures contract, or you might buy a put option, as this would allow you the option to sell the stock, or "put" it, at the option strike price agreed. If the stock did not decline, the hedge would have cost you the option premium. However, if the stock did decline as expected, exercising the option would ensure you did not have to take the loss. This technique is known as a "protective put." Effectively, the cost of the option can be viewed as an insurance premium against loss of value.

You will find the protective put is commonly used, particularly when stocks have reached new highs and investors are fearful the level cannot be maintained. As the option costs a premium, it is not free to protect the value of your portfolio in this way, so the possible benefits must be weighed against the expenses.

Speculation

First, a word about speculation and gambling: These are not the same, and the difference is more than a state of mind or whether the money is spent in the markets or in Las Vegas. Gambling is fundamentally a game of chance, depending on random events, such as the turn of a card or which slot a tiny metal ball will land in on a roulette wheel. Of course, some casino games, such as poker, have elements of skill and intuition, particularly those games that involve interaction with other players, and this brief summary of the differences is not meant to imply all gamblers lack skill and rely on chance for their success. However, speculation is much more clearly a calculated operation.

Speculation should never be entered into in a random manner. There is a wealth of data available about the markets and their characteristics, and it is up to the speculator to determine the important factors. It is a calculated risk the speculator will take for the promise of larger profits.

Speculation is opposite to hedging in trading derivatives. Hedging is meant to manage overall finances to reduce risk, and speculation is meant to invite calculated risk to potentially profit from it. Speculation does not have to involve derivatives, but using leveraged products increases the potential payout and makes speculation much more attractive. Effectively, using leveraged products means using borrowed money to increase the stakes, which means more profit for less investment.

A simple example is that of a breakfast cereal manufacturer that secures the price of the grains it uses months in advance by taking out futures contracts. This is hedging, which may or not work out cheaper than buying the grains when needed. The manufacturer is not concerned with the possibility of saving a few dollars if another possible outcome is costs will soar or grains will not be available for production. The speculator, on the other hand, may take this contract with a knowledge of the crop production expected, the long-range weather forecast, and a reasonable expectation to make a profit.

The Disadvantages

The thing that makes derivatives so attractive for speculators can also be a disadvantage. Derivatives can be successful because of the leverage available, but if the trade goes in the wrong direction, the same leverage acts against the trader and can decimate his or her account.

There are many examples of "mistaken trades," and some have had dramatic effects. Chapter 2 talked about the history of derivatives, and some of the great disasters of the 20th and 21st centuries were mentioned. The demise of Barings Bank came about because of bad trades, which were compounded in an effort to recover the original position. The leverage available with derivatives means it is easy and quick to take on more risk than is wise, and using them requires greater discipline in trading than needed when trading in the stock markets.

Another disadvantage for traders who take an interest in the stock markets through CFDs or single stock futures is they do not own the shares. If they had invested in shares the traditional way, they would be able to take part in the Annual General Meeting and have their voices heard in the running of the company. Instead, they are outsiders and have interests in the performance of a company in which they have zero control.

Perhaps a disadvantage, perhaps not, the practice of marking-to-market certainly influences the trading of derivatives. In some circumstances, it can give you more flexibility to advance your investing agenda. To be able to take profits from your account without even selling the underlying securities and to reinvest or use them for more trading is a bonus, as long as you do not overstretch your resources. The other side — that you may have to keep paying margin amounts into your account to cover a falling price — will certainly make you view derivative trading differently from simply buying and selling shares.

Although the underlying financial instruments can be analyzed and their impact on the derivatives can be projected, it is important to always remember you are not trading the underlying. For instance, CFDs may be traded for profit using technical analysis in a similar way to stock analysis, the way many traders will approach the selection. You would not want to view CFDs as the same as stocks because of the daily interest charged in holding a margined position. Thus, you would not "buy-and-hold" CFDs in the same way you do stocks. They are a trading vehicle.

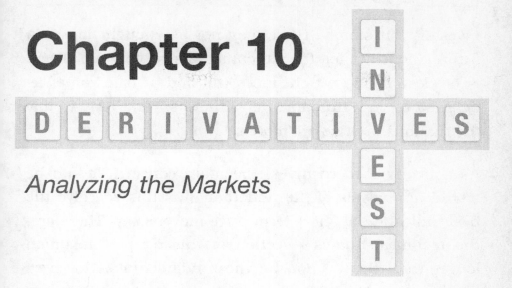

Chapter 10

Analyzing the Markets

Fundamental Analysis: The Basics

In any discussion of trading, the question of fundamental analysis versus technical analysis is bound to come up. In broad terms, fundamental analysis is concerned with the overall health of a company and the economy. It is useful in determining where prices should be, given enough time for the markets to discover them. Technical analysis tends to deal with the day-to-day fluctuations in price charts and, as such, is more directed toward the short-term trader rather than the long-term investor.

Any time you are considering buying something, you will probably do your research to make sure it is a good product. The same applies to the stock market. Do your research, so you are more aware of what you are spending your money on. By their nature, many derivatives have a time element and are better suited to the trader than the investor. Put simply, there may not be enough time in a futures contract for the fundamentals to win out. There is no deadline by which prices will find a "true value" as determined by fundamental analysis, and day-to-day fluctuations in price are more relevant.

As a trader in derivatives, the main concern should be technical analysis of the underlying, as this will give the best indication of short-term price movements. Therefore, the technical analysis section of this chapter is much longer than this section on the fundamentals. However, an understanding of fundamental analysis will ensure you have a firm basis for deciding on the market areas and sectors you will trade. Many traders use fundamental analysis to determine the stocks they should be in and then employ technical analysis to manage timing concerns. Despite short-term trends, if the fundamentals of a particular sector indicate it is unsound, you do not want to trade in it.

Fundamental analysis is not only about individual stocks. It also involves a broad view of the economy in general, the actions of the Federal Reserve, and knowledge of the range of economic indicators and reports issued on a regular basis. The theory of supply and demand underscores much economic activity, and there are many other hypotheses about how the economy runs. The fact that there are so many ideas and economists have many competing theories should indicate no one can really pin down what makes the financial markets tick, but there is general consensus on significant factors.

The Federal Reserve is charged with keeping a stable economy and money supply, and the main tool it has at its command to do this is adjusting the interest rate. The interest rate adjusted is more relevant to banking than to the consumer, but it does have a significant effect on market confidence and the economy in general. Other countries have similar systems to provide regulation; for instance, the Bank of England has a similar function for the United Kingdom.

Western economies are consumer driven. There is a balance that must be struck between providing easy and cheap credit so manufacturing and services industries can sell their products and alternatively making it more difficult to buy things so inflation does not rise. For a healthy economy, it is important for people who want jobs to have them and unemployment is not too high. There are many indicators of these factors, published by the government and independent research groups to give a continuous measure of how a country is doing financially.

Some of these indicators can give rise to moves in the market, and the trader should always be aware of when they will be published if they affect the sector being traded. For instance, the retail price index and reports on consumer sales may affect trading in the retail sector. It is not always clear in what way the numbers will affect the market, as there is an element of anticipation in the prices. If the market has anticipated a bad result, the publishing of the result may not be detrimental if it was not as bad as was expected. These apparent contradictions in the market keep traders guessing and ensure no one can be right all the time.

Depending on the markets you are interested in, the most significant reports to watch include:

- **Gross Domestic Product (GDP):** GDP reflects how well the economy in general is growing, as it adds together the value of all goods and services.

- **Consumer Price Index (CPI):** CPI is watched closely by the Federal Reserve when contemplating changes to the interest rate. It reflects the prices consumers pay for various items and is a set of figures, not just one index number.

- **Producer Price Index (PPI):** The numbers seen for PPI are sometimes a precursor of the CPI because this index is based on the wholesale values the industry is paying.

- **Consumer confidence:** Consumer confidence comprises two reports and is a significant predictor of spending.

- **Housing figures:** Housing figures include the details of the number of housing starts and figures from the National Association of Realtors, which show how many houses have changed hands.

Beyond any consideration of the economy in general, when you are trading, you need to become familiar with the market or sector involved. This will depend on what underlying components you are considering. If you are trading futures on commodities, there are many different ways to approach this question. You may want to become much more familiar with gold mining and refining so your knowledge of the long-term outlook for gold supply can be included in trading gold futures. Agricultural futures cover many different contracts, and many of them can be affected by the weather, which is out of most people's knowledge or control. However, there are many other basic fundamentals, such as what the farmer community in general views as profitable crops to grow and what is being planted, which will feed into your consideration of these futures contracts.

Derivatives are available in many other types of contracts. Perhaps you are attracted by single stock futures, which seems to be an underused type of derivative at the moment. In this case, the fundamentals you need to consider would be concerned with the individual company and its performance, including any management changes, whether the industry is prone to takeovers or management buyouts, and whether the market sector is expected to expand in the future or dwindle.

You will find no shortage of experts online expressing views on the company's latest balance sheets and predicting the long-term future of the business. Numbers to become familiar with include profit and loss, price earnings ratio, capitalization, and other financial statistics. To make analysis easier, be ready to compare the numbers with similar companies in the same sector, so you can decide how competitive and forward thinking the business really is.

If you are more interested in currency speculation, then the fundamentals will involve studying world politics and reviewing the various national numbers, such as unemployment figures and gross domestic products of other countries. Forex trading responds best to technical analysis because you are less likely to uncover unknown fundamental facts about foreign countries than you are about individual companies.

Technical Analysis – A Primer

There are countless trading books written that will give you details of technical analysis. *This rest of this chapter will touch on the myriad of tools and indicators you can use when trading.* If any particular methods of analysis appeal to you investigate them further in books and courses

Technical analysis involves looking at historic trading data, manipulating it, and using the results to predict future price movements. As such, technical analysis is based on the assumption that knowing past price history can give you insight on where prices are headed in the future. Many people believe this, as witness to the number of traders there are in the stock market, though after more than 100 years, you would think traders would have refined their methods to achieve a better success rate. More than 80 percent — and some say more than 90 percent — of beginning traders find they are unable to make a profit and cease trading in the first six months.

Nonetheless, some traders make consistent profits, so it must be assumed the markets are predictable to some extent even though the analysis process is not easy. To the extent trading is carried out by people and people as a whole tend to react in similar ways, a trader should be able to discern a pattern to the way trades happen and, therefore, how people influence the price.

Technical analysis has been developed by many traders over the years and continues to evolve. Above all, it depends on observations of what prices and markets do in response to certain stimuli and then codifying the results to give tradable expectations. One of the most important lessons when beginning to trade is to learn to look at what the market is doing and ignore what you think it should do. The fact is, over the years, people do continue to respond in similar ways, and therefore, it is possible to detect patterns and trends that help to produce successful trades.

It is interesting to observe that technical analysis techniques are portable and can be used across all markets traded in the same way. Thus, if you learn the basics of technical analysis for stock trading, similar methods can be used and applied to forex and other markets.

Dow Theory

The Dow Theory is named after Charles Dow, one of the founders of Dow, Jones & Company. Some say his work created the art and science of technical analysis. He died in 1902 and never actually created the Dow Theory. Instead, he published his observations of the market in *The Wall Street Journal*, which he edited until his death. These observations were later assembled by friends to create what is now known as the Dow Theory.

Up until 1897, there was only one stock average, but at the beginning of that year, there were two averages created, one for industrial or manufacturing stocks and the other for the railroad or transportation. These were termed the Dow Jones Industrial Average (DJIA) and the Dow Jones Transportation Average (DJTA). An important observation of Dow was, if these did not move in the same direction, there was a problem with the markets and the trader should be cautious. "What one makes, the other takes" was Dow's way of expressing it.

Dow's work went on to identify three influences on stock prices. The first was the primary trend lasting several years. The secondary movement would last from three weeks to three months and typically retrace one-third to two-thirds of the previous market action. The third movement was the day-to-day fluctuations.

Dow also identified three stages to each primary trend. For a bull market, it starts with a general movement up, subject to consolidations, but with each rally rising to a peak higher than previous highs. The second stage is when there is increasing volume because of great demand from good business conditions. The final stage is when speculation is rampant and the prices are being pushed up by hope rather than fact. Similarly, in a bear market, the first stage is the abandonment of that hope, the second stage is selling because of lower corporate earnings, and the third stage is distressed selling at any price.

Although the Dow Theory has been criticized over the years for various reasons, such as the fact he only used closing prices, the method was not intended for short-term trading, and it is slow to confirm a trend, its proponents have continued to refine and update it, and there is a strong following on Wall Street for his basic ideas.

Elliott Wave Theory

The Elliott Wave Theory is viewed by some as more of a philosophical approach to markets rather than a theory. It describes a long-term wave pattern and is similar to the Dow Theory in that respect. Ralph Nelson Elliott observed in the 1930s that price action appeared in a wave formation on charts, and he produced a simple theory about movements up and retracements, which in application may become complex. It was popularized by Robert Prechter and A. J. Frost in their book *Elliott Wave Principle* in the 1970s. The hypothesis is each major trip consists of five points of reversal — three upward and two retracements. As daily fluctuations may be responsible for many hesitations or minor retracements, it can take some experience to properly interpret the Elliott Wave pattern. The method has many adherents.

Patterns

These two theories lead us to one of the ways technical analysts try to anticipate the market. In a more general way, some traders rely on identifying patterns in the price chart in order to estimate the future price movement. What is meant by pattern is a particular geometric shape the price of a security will trace on a chart over time. Some of these patterns have easy descriptive titles and some names are more colorful, such as Megaphone Top, Tombstone Bottom, or Prussian Helmet.

Patterns are more effective when used on stocks and financial securities that have a large trading volume, or liquidity. This tends to smooth out the disruptive effects of an odd trade that runs against the general trend. One of the important factors to check, whether your trading method specifically involves calculation with it or not, is the amount of volume traded on the shares. The less volume, the less the price is likely to follow the general rules.

Prices generally do one of three things. They may continue to increase over time subject to minor fluctuations, called an uptrend. They may decline over time, forming a downtrend. Identifying these trends provides obvious trading opportunities. A large amount of the time, perhaps as much as 40 percent, prices do neither of these things but continue to stay at about the same level, trading up and down within a limited range. There are ways to make money with any of these behaviors, but patterns are more generally used to find trading opportunities in a trending market. *This is detailed in Chapter 12.*

Patterns can be divided into two types — continuation patterns, which indicate the trend will continue, and reversal patterns, which denote a possible change from one trend to the other, such as from a downtrend to an uptrend. The reversal patterns are usually emphasized because they present the best opportunities for large profits. Even so, as price movements tend to have far fewer reversals than continuations, both types of patterns are useful to the trader.

By way of example, one well-known reversal pattern is called the Head and Shoulders Pattern. It also happens to be one of the most reliable chart patterns. It is named for the way it looks on a chart: It has three peaks and two troughs. The middle peak is the highest and represents the head, and the peaks on each side are called the shoulders. The troughs between form the neckline.

The head and shoulders pattern may develop during a bull market, which is an uptrend, and it forecasts a reversal to a downtrending price. Although it is relatively reliable, traders usually look for other factors, such as a decreasing volume of trading for each successive peak, and expect the reversal to be confirmed when the price drops by at least 3 percent below the neckline, which is when they would make their entry. This 3-percent rule is due to Robert

Edwards and John Magee in their seminal work *Technical Analysis of Stock Trends* and has proved a good general rule over time.

Many other patterns have been identified and are watched for by traders. Unlike other trading indications, patterns are one aspect of technical analysis at which the human eye has been better than the computer.

Plotting charts

One of the basic tools for the technical analyst is the price chart, and three variations are shown as an example. There are some more specialized ways of presenting the data, but the complexities of these are beyond an appendix.

Figure 3: Line Chart

The first price chart simply shows the line indicating the closing market price of the share each day. There is one price for each day or each period, as these charts can be produced with different time scales. Short-term traders commonly use daily charts, day traders can use charts with periods down to five minutes, and longer times are used to look at historical trends. From a chart like this, traders can see whether the price has been tending to go up or down in the last few weeks.

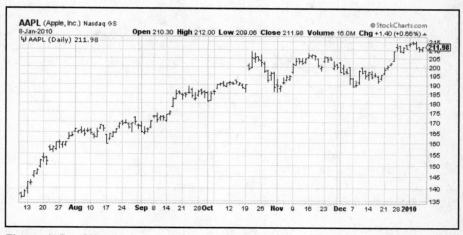

Figure 4: Bar Chart

More information needed to be shown in the same size chart, so the Western bar chart (Figure 4) was invented. So called because each day is represented by a vertical bar, the chart actually contains four pieces of price information for each day. If you look closely, you can see each bar has a short horizontal tick to the left, and one to the right.

The four pieces of information include the price the stock first traded at when the market opened, the final price traded before the close, and the lowest and highest prices traded during the day. The bar itself stretches from the lowest price to the highest price; the tick to the left is at the opening price, and the tick to the right is at the closing price. This provides a lot more information for the trader, including whether the price rose or fell during the day and how volatile the price has been.

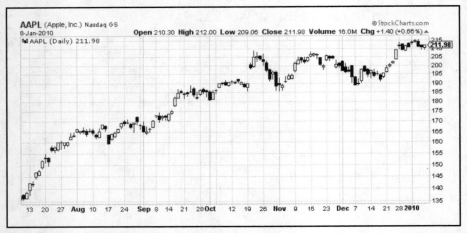

Figure 5: Candlestick Chart

The further development of this chart is shown in Figure 5, which is called a candlestick chart because the symbol for each day looks like a candle. This form of graphing was used in Japan for hundreds of years but was not used in the Western world until the late 1980s, when Steve Nison, now acknowledged as the father of candlestick charts in the West, researched and introduced it to the markets. Due to the graphical nature, the candlestick chart has all but supplanted the bar chart, even though it contains the same information.

Each "candle" is made up of a fat section, called the real body; a line upwards from the body called the upper wick; and a line downwards, which is the lower wick. Depending on the numbers being depicted, sometimes these three candle elements may be smaller or larger, and in the case of the wicks, may not show at all.

The real body stretches from the opening price to the closing price, and the wicks extend further to mark the lowest and highest prices of the session. The clever part is if the price has risen from open to close, the real body is white, or on colored charts green, and if the price has fallen over the day, the real body is black or sometimes red. This gives an instant indication at first glance of the daily price trend.

There have been many books written about interpreting the hundreds of candlestick patterns, a powerful indication of market sentiment. For this discussion, it should be noted if the real body is long, it suggests strong and decisive price action by the market. If the real body is short, or perhaps just a horizontal line, which is called a Doji and indicates opening and closing prices were the same, it tends to indicate market indecision and possible reversal. Candlestick patterns should never be taken on their own as trading signals, but can yield valuable information about where the price should go next.

CASE STUDY: KEEN ON CANDLESTICKS

Mark Deaton
www.candlestickgenius.com

Mark Deaton is based in Idaho. He enjoys hunting, fishing, time with family, and trading the markets. He is a big fan of using candlesticks in his trading and maintains an educational site that has become popular for people who want to learn about how to use candlestick patterns in their trading. For more information on Deaton, visit his website, www.candlestickgenius.com.

I trade options on ETFs and stocks. I trade straight calls and puts as well as vertical spreads, Iron Condors, and other more complex strategies.

I prefer the advanced spread strategies because they require less work in managing the trades. I can oftentimes put on trades that need no attention for two to three weeks. I am a busy guy; the less work the better.

I was led to trade derivatives purely for the upside potential: the leverage. Of course, as I learned early on, the downside was equal to the upside.

The current financial situation has certainly slowed my actual trading of options on specific stocks because they are so volatile with any news. I have actually traded more ETFs now than I ever have. Additionally, I have spent more time than usual in the forex section of my platform.

The most exciting part about derivatives is getting in on a trade, being right in your assessment, and exiting with 100 percent — or even 350 percent — in profits in a short amount of time. Equally as exciting is having a trade go against you aggressively and managing your exit to a tiny profit or small loss. Getting out of a bad trade unscathed is a lot of fun.

What I dislike most about derivatives is bid versus ask spreads. I hate when I wait patiently for a perfect setup and the market makers have decided to make it next to impossible to make a profit. When the markets are in turmoil and uncertain, the powers that be put a huge spread between the bid and ask so even if price rockets in your direction, some simple math will tell you, you will not make any money.

What personal qualities do I think help? Patience is important. I have some bad habits I brought with me into trading. The good news is you do not have to learn the hard way. Stick to paper trading first. Quit looking for the "Holy Grail;" it does not exist. Just exercise patience and utilize a simple approach. Do not let a series of successful trades give you unrealistic confidence. Lock in profits and put some time and effort into your exit. It is more important than your entry.

My biggest success? My best trade ever was a trade I entered on AAPL in April of 2009. It was simple logic that had me in the trade: a violation of a swing high. I made the decision to quit ignoring long signals because I was bearish at heart like the rest of the world. I jumped in with a 90-day call option that I rolled up a few more times before exiting with very large profits. That run turned out to be one of the strongest bull runs in many years. Had I followed more long signals, I would have made a small fortune.

My biggest challenge is when I pick a side — bearish or bullish — and I start ignoring the signals from the other side. Remaining neutral and letting the markets tell me bearish or bullish has always been difficult for me. This has cost me more money in passed opportunities than I can even count. These were times where I saw the signal and the trigger but skipped the trade because of my bearish or bullish bias.

If someone wanted to follow in my footsteps, I would tell him or her to learn to stay neutral and let price action determine outlook. Master the simple, yet powerful, topic of swing lows and highs and support and resistance. Develop a simple system that uses these key tools and let everything else you employ simply support these.

Charts are available with the prices, the vertical scale shown as either linear or logarithmic. It is a matter of personal preference, but many people advise using the logarithmic scale because it gives a better indication of price movements. On the logarithmic scale, the distance between any two numbers depends on the ratio between the two numbers and not the arithmetic difference. This means if the price doubles from two to four, the distance on the price chart is the same as when the price doubles from four to eight or ten to 20.

Support and resistance

Another fundamental part of technical analysis is trying to determine support and resistance levels on the chart. These usually denote pricing areas where it is important to make a trading decision.

In basic terms, support is a price level where a declining security may be expected to stop falling in price, which will be supported at that level by buyers wanting to own the stock. A resistance level is the opposite — the price at which the value of a rising stock will stop increasing as sellers dump the stock and take their profits.

In real life, it is not always easy to identify the support and resistance levels, and it is worth looking at weekly or monthly charts to see the overall pattern. If the support level is identified and the price comes down to it, it may be reasonable to assume the price will start rising again. The trader will normally wait to see if the price drops through the support because if it does, it may be a sign the market sentiment has changed, and the price will not recover as expected. If the price starts to increase from the support, it might make a good trade.

Resistance can be used in the same way. If the stock price rises and then starts declining from the level of resistance, it may be worth trading the stock short. When the price goes between the support and resistance repeatedly, trading in a limited range, it can be called range bound, and trading between the limits can make some money.

After a period of range-bound trading, the stock price may penetrate either the support or resistance, called a breakout. Once the support or resistance does not hold, you may expect the price to move further. The toughest decision is to determine whether the breakout is real or just a minor fluctuation. The trader will want to get in on the move as early as possible for the biggest gains, but jumping too early can lead to losses.

An interesting observation is when the stock price has broken out, the previous resistance level becomes a new support level for the higher price.

Moving averages

Before considering the more complex indicators invented to assist in technical analysis, first look at the simple moving average. This can be used to signal trading, set profit targets, and indicate whether you should be trading at all. With all the other complex indicators at their disposal, some traders tend to overlook the flexibility of the family of moving averages, but there are powerful techniques that use them.

A moving average is a line plotted on the chart that shows the average of the previous X number of days, where X is any number. What value you place on X depends on what you want to do with the moving average. The relationship between the current price and the moving average will have significance, depending on the trading system being followed.

There are several types of moving averages available, with the basic one called the simple moving average (SMA). Another one frequently encountered is the exponential moving average (EMA). The only difference between the various types of moving averages is the importance assigned to different price data. The EMA gives more importance, or weight, to more recent figures. Recognizing any moving average lags the current price action, such weighting is an attempt to make the average more current.

In its simplest form, a trading plan could be to buy a stock when its price rises above a moving average and sell it if the price drops below the average. This will not maximize the profit, but it does have the advantage of ensuring you are always trading with the trend. A 200-day or 39-week moving average is commonly used for this and as a general trend indicator as well. If the moving average is sloping upwards, the price is in an uptrend.

Moving averages can be used as support and resistance. With this concept, instead of drawing straight lines for support and resistance, the trader lets the moving average line show the reversal level. The key to this technique is to determine the optimal time period for the moving average, done by reviewing the relationship between the moving average and price line over a long period. In many ways, this is better than using fixed support and resistance levels because in the real world, prices may not move in a straight line.

Each individual stock and commodity will have its own cyclical pattern, which means it is hard to generalize which is the best moving average time period to use. It is possible to give a general indication or starting point for experimentation and try testing moving averages with the following values of X to indicate support and resistance levels:

- For stock indices such as the S&P 500, many traders use the 50-day moving average for short-term support and resistance. For investment purposes and the longer term, analysts tend to use the 200-day moving average. As these are widely traded indices and many institutional investors use these numbers, you will find they are fairly accurate and, to some extent, self-fulfilling.

- For actively traded individual stocks, try starting with a 30-day moving average on the daily chart or a 30-week moving average for weekly charts. These numbers produce good results with a large number of different stocks.

- If you are interested in commodities, a shorter time period will work better. For agricultural commodities, 9-day and 18-day moving averages are a good starting point for daily charts, using 9-week and 18-week moving averages on weekly charts.

Indicators

There are many different technical indicators available, which confirms the fact there is no perfect answer to finding profitable trades all the time. However, they have their place in the technical analysts' repertoire and can provide clues to the question of when to trade. It is never a good practice to trade based on one indicator or pattern, but what you are looking for is corroboration between different measures of the market.

Many indicators are developed to attempt to anticipate market movements. Moving averages are inevitably lagging, despite having their uses, and mathematical manipulations of the pricing data can result in indicators that seem almost to have captured the power of prediction. Many of these indicators are available at online charting websites, such as StockCharts.com (**www.stockcharts.com**), and usually at the broker's websites, so you can practice your trading skills and develop your trading plan before committing to a major expenditure.

Most indicators are shown below the price chart, unlike the moving average and support and resistance lines. Many give indications of whether the stock may be considered overbought, which means the upward pressure on the price may not be maintained, and the price may fall, or be oversold, which would equate to the start of an uptrend, if correct.

One of the best-known indicators for traders is the Moving Average Convergence Divergence (MACD) indicator, based on moving averages, but as the name suggests, develops the idea by considering the convergence or divergence of two moving average lines of different periods. The crossing point of two different moving average lines may be considered a trading signal in some trading systems. The MACD attempts to preempt that signal on the obvious basis that before the averages cross, they must converge.

Another well-known trading indicator is the Stochastic Oscillator. This gives clear indications of overbought or oversold conditions calculated from its equations. The principle, taken care of by the charting computer, is to compare a stock's closing price with the range of prices experienced. If the closing prices are in the higher ranges, this is an indication of an upward trend; when the closing prices are at the lower end of the price range, it indicates lack of interest in the price level and possible downtrend.

The last major indicator to be mentioned here is the Relative Strength Indicator. This shows overbought and oversold conditions and can also be used for a trading signal based on direction or crossing a certain level. The relative strength in the title can be confusing, as it does not refer to the stock's strength in comparison to other securities; rather, it measures the strength of the price movement relative to previous movements in the stock's price.

There are many other indicators, but it is seldom a trader will use more than two or three at a time. Implementation comes down to experimentation and personal preference. The only caveat is to say to select indicators that are complementary and not based on the same part of the pricing data. For instance, the RSI is based on price momentum, so it could be used with another indicator based on moving averages.

Technical analysis with commodities

When you are trading stocks, certain parameters apply. When you are trading in equities, you can sell at a loss if you have mistaken the position. Trading commodities involves trading on hope, and futures have only a limited time span. It is easy to lose all the money you have put up on margin. Therefore, technical analysis is even more important with commodities than with equities. Correct timing, which analysis can help with, is paramount.

Some basics are the same. For instance, follow trend lines and look for breakouts to signal buy or sell points. However, as much as 80 percent of trading is for commercial hedging and not speculation, and this means short-term support and resistance levels have less significance than with stocks. Commercial demands may require trading beyond those arbitrary boundaries often adhered to by stock traders.

Using the volume in your technical analysis is more difficult with commodities than with stocks. With stocks, there are a limited number of shares and every transaction involves change of ownership. With commodities, there is no limit to the number of contracts, and the number of contracts may not even be related to the expected harvest. Open interest, the number of contracts traded, may be much more than the actual supply when the expiration date occurs.

Some elements of stock pricing are much more easily predicted than elements affecting commodity futures pricing. For example, profits and price earnings ratios are matters good management can influence and control. Elements affecting commodities can include weather, particularly with the recognition of climate change, global warming, and political and international matters.

Technical analysis with options

In discussing the pricing of options, the stock prices are closely linked with the option prices. That means technical analysis on the stock charts is key to making profitable plays in options.

There is money to be made with writing options, which is taking the opposite position to the buyer. You will be paid a premium as soon as the option is bought, and this is the principle behind writing covered calls, where with good fortune, you can receive a periodic income while holding on to your shares. *This is discussed more in Chapter 12.* Some speculators consider writing naked calls, or selling a call without owning the stock. This is a chancy business and is best not considered.

Chapter 11

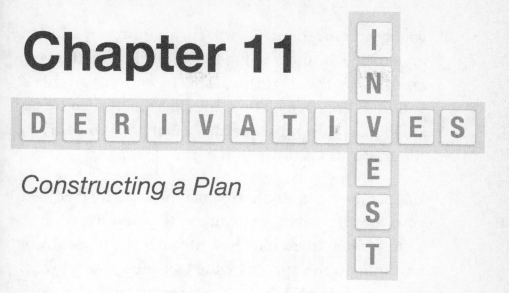

DERIVATIVES

Constructing a Plan

Trading Guidelines

Whenever you are contemplating trading for a profit, whether it involves derivatives, forex, or just plain equities, there are some important overall principles to bear in mind for improving chances of success. If you do not follow these, you may find your trading career is short lived.

- Never trade with money you cannot afford to lose. Whether it is money you need for next month's mortgage payment or savings to replace your car in a few years, it is a mistake to use money to which you are so emotionally connected. Emotions are the downfall of many prospective traders.

- Be prepared to cut losses quickly if the trade turns against you. It is natural to believe your analysis was good and the trade will turn around. But there is no place for that feeling in the market, as the best analysis in the world can still be proved wrong. If you find it hard to exit a trade that has turned into a small loss, how much harder will it be if you stay in the trade and it turns into a large loss?

- Do not be in a rush to take profits; instead, let your profits run. Particularly if you have had a losing trade, there may be a strong urge to exit from a winning trade and enjoy the fact you made a profit. Although you should look after your money, it does not make sense to cash in while the trade is still making money. Consider, instead, tightening up your stop loss position.

- Rarely — most traders say never — trade against the trend. There may be some profits to be made if you time a retracement move, but the odds are against doing this consistently. Trading is all about putting the odds on your side so you make steady profits. If you are looking for a few stellar trades to set you up for retirement, you are playing the lottery and not trading.

- Do not think you always have to be trading, even if you cannot find a good place for your money. Depending on your style, there may be no suitable trades, and forcing the issue is likely to be problematic.

- Do not enter a trade just because it looks cheap. There may be a good reason why people are shunning it. Values can be found, but do your homework and do not expect profits to fall into your lap.

- When you are learning to trade, your primary objective is to protect your capital. If you lose your money, you will be unable to trade. If you concentrate on not losing the account rather than on making gains, you will be much more successful.

CASE STUDY: THE IMPORTANCE OF A PLAN

Mike Ryske
Stock option trader
Mike@netpicks.com
www.netpicks.com

I have been trading for almost seven years. I got hooked on the markets in college while researching a project for a business class. The markets have fascinated me since. I got my start in trading options, and though I have branched out into the futures markets as well, swing trading options remains my specialty. Over the past two years, I have been a trading coach for NetPicks, where I help traders overcome the many obstacles that can come up while trading.

My journey as a retail trader has helped me teach many traders how to get the most out of their trading. I have made all the same mistakes they will make, which is the best tool I think I can use. They are able to see I was in their shoes seven years ago. Becoming a successful trader does not require an advanced degree, just a dedication to learn as much as possible.

I prefer to buy and sell options on single stocks over the index products or exchange-traded funds. I want to follow stocks I am very familiar with, so my watch list focuses on the big names traders see in the news on a daily basis. This means my watch list is not large and does not come from any scanning software. My watch list typically contains fewer than 15 stocks. This allows me to be familiar with the options pricing and levels of volatility. Although index products and ETFs have proven to be nice trading vehicles, I do not find them to fit my style as well as single stocks.

Stock options provide a great way for the retail trader to get involved with higher-priced stocks such as Apple or Google with smaller account sizes because of the leverage options provide. Getting involved in a higher-priced stock can tie up massive amounts of capital for the smaller stock trader. Options allow that smaller trader to get in with less of their capital at risk, which also provides a way of implementing better risk management rules.

Due to the lower cost of initiating a position with options as opposed to stock, the trader has the potential to see nice returns on a percentage basis. A small move in the stock can produce some impressive returns in a short amount of time.

When I started trading, I was interested in markets and systems that would allow me to trade actively with a smaller account size. When I found options, they fit my style perfectly. I am more of a conservative trader who likes to think two steps ahead before I get into a trade. Trading options gives me the flexibility to apply different strategies to different market conditions. When only trading stocks, you have two plays: You can buy or you can sell. When trading the same stock using options, you have strategies that can take advantage of volatility and time decay (spread trading), which allow you to take advantage of the current market environment.

I am often asked how the current financial situation has affected my trading on a regular basis. They are always surprised to hear the current financial situation has provided some of the best trading conditions of my career. The increased levels of volatility provide opportunities to profit with options on moves to the upside and downside. Options give you the ability to adapt to different market conditions, so the increased levels of volatility due the uncertainty in the economy have given traders the chance to profit from these moves we have seen.

Trading options gets exciting when you are able to see 70 to 100 percent return on your capital in a short amount of time. I can control a nice-sized position of Apple stock, for example, while staying below my maximum risk per trade of 2 percent of my account. Purchasing a single call option can give me control of 100 shares of Apple stock for typically under a few thousand dollars, while establishing that same 100-share position on just the stock would cost approximately $20,000. As a retail trader, trading derivatives allows me to participate in markets that before were only available to larger institutional traders.

What frustrates me most about trading derivatives is how many traders use them incorrectly, which can give derivatives a bad reputation. Being a trading coach at NetPicks allows me to work with traders on a regular basis, and it really bothers me to see so many people blowing out accounts because they don't understand the products they are trading. Trading options involves more than just picking a stock and buying a call or a put. You have to understand what it is you are doing when putting that position on. Although the leverage these products offer is great, if not used correctly, the losses can add up very quickly. Proper risk management is crucial to trading options successfully.

As a trader, discipline is absolutely essential. Being involved with sports my entire life really provided the foundation for me to become a disciplined trader. Many times, new traders get drawn in by the promise of easy wealth without understanding what it takes to become profitable. I learned the hard way that there are thousands of traders out there who are more than willing to take your money if you do not stay disciplined to the plan you have laid out for yourself. That plan starts with finding a system that gives you an edge and then creating rules for yourself that you follow religiously each trading day. Trading like a gunslinger can be exciting but will eventually lead to an empty account every time.

The most profitable trade of my career also happens to be the reason I struggled to find consistency early on. I established a position of Yahoo! calls just before earnings were to be released the following day.

The earnings came out great, and the stock soared the next day, which lead to me booking a very large winner with my options. Unfortunately, I had no valid reason for placing the trade other than a hunch earnings were going to beat estimates. This immediately led to bad habits. I had no plan in place. I was just shooting from the hip. I talk about this trade often with my coaching students to show how a profitable trade does not always mean you are a successful trader.

My biggest challenge as a trader is the direct result of my biggest success. Bad habits are so easily formed. I had a massive win with my Yahoo! Trade, which led me to believe trading options was an easy occupation. My thinking was, "Why do I need a system when I can book winners like this without any help?" This led to a few years of very inconsistent results. Becoming a successful trader is a result of establishing rules for myself after each mistake I made along the way. Today, I will not put a dime of my capital to work if I do not have a detailed trade plan in place for that given market. I need to know exactly where I am getting in, where I am getting out, and how I am going to manage the position once I am in it. Finding a trading system that gives you all of these specific levels is crucial to becoming a profitable options trader.

I would advise new traders that trading options can give you more flexibility than any other occupation out there; however, you have to be willing to put in the time to create processes for yourself. As a retail trader, you do not have anyone there telling you what to do every minute of the day, which is great. The problem with this is you do not have anyone there to tell you what to do every minute of the day. In other words, no one is there to hold you accountable. This is why it is crucial you become a disciplined trader. I would highly recommend finding a trading coach who can walk alongside you initially to make sure you are following your own rules. Make sure you have a documented trading plan in place before you even think about trading with live funds. There is no way around spending the hours testing a market or a system in order to build that trade plan in which you can be confident. Becoming a successful trader will only come once you are able to be disciplined day in and day out.

Money Management

Lack of good money management is one of the major reasons many traders fail. Often traders allow emotions to take over and overthrow careful plans for entering and exiting trades. The previous point summarizes this sentiment and gives the reason for good money management. There are a number of rules and guidelines to comply with to retain control of your finances.

Whenever entering into a trade, be aware already of how much profit you expect to make and at what point you will exit the trade if it starts losing. Traders usually expect to have a minimum of a three to one ratio between the expected reward and the possible loss, often called the risk/reward ratio. If you always enter trades where if you win, you gain more than you stand to lose, you can afford to win less than half the time, which stacks the odds in favor of making a long-term profit.

Traders refer to a stop loss position, the price at which they will get out of a trade going wrong. As mentioned in the previous paragraph, for a viable trade, the possible loss should be much less than the possible gain. It is important to know where your stop loss position will be if your trade is losing. This is not something you calmly decide after having entered a trade, as your emotions are immediately involved. Besides, if you have not figured it out before trading, you cannot know if your risk/reward ratio is favorable. Some trades are not worth taking out, even if the entry signals are clear.

The key element in making consistent profits is the size of all the losses compared with the size of all the profits. Even if you identify winning trades 80 percent of the time — not many traders would claim to be able to do this — if you do not control your losses and fail to let your profits run, you may still find your account diminishing.

That being said, the next consideration is how large your trades should be, called position sizing. As a general rule, many traders say no more than 10 percent of your trading account should go into any trading position. You must limit the amount you risk losing on every trade you enter. This is done principally by considering where your stop loss is placed and how large a trade you will make.

Depending on your trading method, the market or the charts will dictate a prudent position for your stop loss. It is then a matter of working backward from your risk amount to determine how much to buy. The risk amount is normally represented as a percentage of your trading account, and good practice normally dictates this is no more than 2 percent.

This may sound like just a little, but bear in mind it does not represent how much money you are putting into the trade — only how much you will lose if the trade turns against you. You can calculate your potential losses from your stop loss position. This process is known as position sizing, as mentioned above.

Making the Plan

Not many traders would say to avoid a detailed plan when trading. You will usually find these few traders have "paid their dues" many times over while they were learning and have developed an instinct that permits them to make such a claim. They are the exception, as most of their generation, if they had the same attitude, will have lost a significant amount and given up trading.

Much better advice is to have a detailed plan and then try hard to stick with it. It may sound strange to talk about sticking with a plan if you have not traded before, but it is a common experience that the emotions of trading with your own real money can distort your thinking and make you deviate from your intentions of following a plan.

The next chapter details some particular strategies, many suited for options because of the particular features and challenges they have, and some more ideas for futures, but the basics of trading are well established. For general trading purposes in many of the other derivatives, if you are looking at the value of a particular security, then you can use technical analysis on a price chart and form a good opinion of which way the price is going to move.

Primarily, look for an established trend, whether a rising trend or a declining price. Be warned about half the time, most securities do not have a definite up or down trend, but the price meanders around the same level. This is sometimes called trending sideways, or trendless activity. When seeing if a trend is established, always check on different times on the chart, as they can sometimes yield different pictures.

Even with a strongly trending security, there are times when the price pulls back, almost as if it is catching its breath before another spurt in the main direction. A popular trading strategy is to buy as soon as the pullback appears to be finished, and your trading plan should define how you determine this, whether by observation of the price resuming the trend or by using a particular indicator or oscillator. This can be applied to uptrending and downtrending markets.

Another tactic that could form the basis of a trading plan would be to buy stocks or securities that exhibit a high strength relative to the rest of the market. In this case, you might specify a stock performing "x" percent better than the overall market and "y" percent better than its market sector. Such performance defines an upward trending stock, and you could go long while it still showed this superior performance.

The other side of this type of trading plan would be to go short or sell on relative weakness, which you could find in a similar way by comparing the overall figures.

If you are the type who wants to stay "hands on" all the time, also explore the possibility of trading in a sideways trend. This has the advantage of being in the market most of the time, and you still have a strategy for trading even when you do not have a definite uptrend or downtrend. The disadvantage of trading sideways is you will not get large gains from a major trend move but instead are looking for many small and repetitive gains. You will be trading within a limited range.

This method of trading, sometimes called buying support and selling resistance, involves looking for a security fluctuating between two distinct price levels. As noted in Chapter 10, these are called the support and resistance, and they define boundary levels the price is having difficulty going beyond. The more times the fluctuating price has touched these levels and turned back, the better the confirmation that they are relevant.

As you are not following a long trend but trading on the regular fluctuations in price, these trades are likely to be short lived. When the price comes down to support, you would go long in the security and, you hope, watch as it rises up toward resistance before taking a profit. From the resistance level, you would go short and profit as the price sinks.

This method of trading has the risk the price will "break out" of the trading range and catch you on the wrong side of the trade. Therefore, if you try this method, stay alert and on top of the price action.

Your trading plan must include details of your initial stop loss position. This should not be considered discretionary. If you have the software and can back test your plan, which is highly recommended, you will need to detail where your stop loss will be placed so the back testing can include failed trades that were stopped out. Some traders will place their stop loss according to a percentage or certain value away from the entry price.

This is an acceptable starting point but has the disadvantage that different financial instruments have different volatilities, and volatility can change over time, which requires specific back testing on this security to check on the sensitivity to adjusting this value. Another method more closely related to the actual volatility is setting the stop loss a multiple of the average true range (ATR) away from the price, as this takes into account the security's actual trading pattern. ATR is available on most charts.

Once you have a position open and moving in the right direction, you may wish to set a trailing stop loss to help preserve any profits made. You will find it helpful to write down all these details before you start so you will not forget any critical aspect.

Whichever type of trading appeals to you, start with a written plan that is unambiguous. Taking away your own discretion will provide consistent results and allow you to back test your plan so you can optimize the numbers for the best results.

Another highly recommended notion is to keep a trading journal. This can be hand written, or stored on the computer, whichever you find easier to do, as the point is not the format but that you take action to record matters as your trading progresses. The trading journal gives not only details of the trades you make, tabulated with prices and times, but also should include your feelings at the time and your reasons for making the trade. This gives you a sound basis from which to review your performance and determine what weak spots you may need to work on.

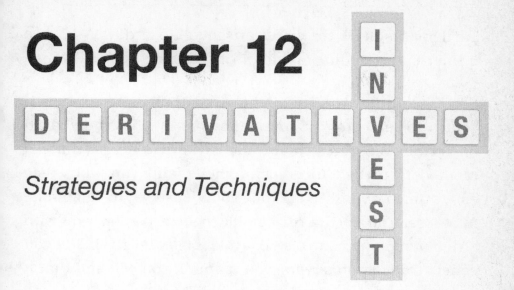

Chapter 12

DERIVATIVES

Strategies and Techniques

There are a number of strategies that have emerged over the years that allow you to make full use of the particular features of different derivatives. Chapter 11 covered general ways financial securities may be traded, and this is applicable to any derivative that reflects the securities price directly, such as contracts for difference. In such a case, the chief benefit of using a derivative is the leverage obtained.

Make full use of back testing when deciding on your strategy. There are many indicators and analysis tools available, many more than have been mentioned in the technical analysis section, and more are being invented all the time. Some, such as moving averages and Bollinger bands, can give you price targets. Others are meant to indicate the sympathy of the market — whether the market participants think the prices are going up or down — to see if the trend is ending and about to reverse.

Some securities are better behaved than others when it comes to indicators. Some indicators are better behaved on certain securities than others. There is no guaranteed method to predict future movement, and you will waste your time trying to refine your system to eliminate mistakes. You need a reasonable system you operate with strict monetary controls to avoid big losses, and if you concentrate on preserving your capital, you will find that it increases naturally over the course of trading.

Aside from predicting market values, other types of derivatives, such as options, present different challenges and opportunities, and a completely new set of trading strategies have been developed to allow full use of these features. *Thus, there is an emphasis on optionfeatures in this chapter, and this chapter details techniques more specific to derivative trading than general trading advice.*

Exercising American Options

As you will recall from the discussion on options in Chapter 5, there are two basic styles. The European option can only be exercised on the expiration date. It does not matter if this option has been in the money prior to expiry; you will only profit if it is in the money at expiration. The American option, on the other hand, can be exercised any time up to the expiration. If the day after you buy a call option the value of the underlying increases greatly, you can immediately demand to buy it at the option strike price. Whether the option is a European style or an American style does not necessarily follow from where you live or which market you bought it on, and be clear before entering the contract what type of option you are getting.

The obvious question arising from these facts is how do you determine whether to exercise an American option early to maximize your profit? What is the optimal strategy you should use to calculate when desiring to take an early profit if you are trading an American option? After all, you can expect to pay more for an American option because of the additional flexibility it offers, so you want to be sure you make the most of it.

That said, you may be surprised to hear it is not considered wise to exercise an American call option early, except sometimes if the stock is dividend paying. This does not mean you necessarily allow the option to run its course to expiration without taking any other action, but there are strategies you need to be aware of that can lock in or increase your gains.

The strategies are best explained by giving you examples. Start with the basic assumption that you hold ten American call options in a stock trading at $100 and your options have a strike price of $80, so they are well in the money. The options do not expire for two months. You may be tempted to cash them in now, just in case the stock price falls.

If you exercise the options right away, you will be buying 1,000 shares, as each option covers 100 shares, at a price of $80,000, and the shares are worth $100,000. You may be tempted to take this $20,000 profit (less than the original option cost) and feel good about your trade.

The first and most obvious thing to consider is you can sell your options for more than $20,000. In Chapter 8, it was pointed out an option is worth the sum of its intrinsic value and its time value. $20,000 is the intrinsic value of your options, and with two months left to run, there is without doubt some time value as well.

If you exercised your options and sold the shares immediately, you would only gain the intrinsic value of $20,000. If you kept hold of the shares, you would run the risk of them falling in value and losing the gains you were hoping for. So, in either case, selling the options will work out better.

If you are unable to sell your options, you could invest the $80,000 you were going to use to exercise at a risk-free rate of interest. If, by the expiration date, the stock price is still above the strike price, cash in the investment and buy the stock for $80,000, and you will have gained two months interest on your money. If, by the expiration date, the stock is trading for less than $80, again, cash in your investment and buy the stock, and you profit by the interest and by how much the stock was under the strike price. In either case, you are better off than if you had exercised the option two months previously and held the stock.

It may be you believe the stock price has reached a peak and is bound to fall before the expiration date. You may think your best choice of action would be to exercise the option and sell the stock immediately to lock in the gains in the intrinsic value. Once again, there is another course that would work out better for you.

If you think the stock price is going to go down, the better choice would be to sell the stock short. If you are correct, you will make money from your short position as the price falls. Even if the price only goes down to the strike price, your short position will have locked in your gains. However, if you are wrong and the stock continues to rise, you still have the opportunity to exercise the option at expiration. You will have lost on your short position any additional gains over and above the initial gains but will have still made the same profit as if you had exercised the option early.

As mentioned, the one exception to not exercising the American call option early may be for a dividend-paying stock. In this case, it may be best to exercise just before the dividend payment, so as a stockholder, you are paid the dividend. It depends on a calculation of how large the dividend will be compared with the option value and the interest you could have been earning on the money to buy the stocks.

When considering an American put option, it can occasionally be worthwhile to exercise before expiration. Perhaps the stock has tanked and is trading near zero, you have a reasonable strike price, and it is unlikely the stock will trade up again. In this circumstance, you may as well exercise the put option and get the money now. The stock price cannot go below zero, and the money received from the option can be put to good use earning interest.

Covered Call

One of the better-known options strategies is called the covered call. If you have been trading for any time, you have probably heard of it. It involves writing a call option, which means you must supply the underlying shares at the strike price if the option is exercised.

The term "covered" means you already own the shares to meet your obligation — you are not vulnerable to price surprises. If the option is exercised, you just have to sell your shares to the option buyer at the strike price. The alternative is called a "naked" call option, used when you do not hold the shares and are totally exposed to market forces and price variations. If the option is exercised, you would be forced to buy the shares at the market price in order to fulfill your obligation. Because of this, naked call writing is rightly considered one of the riskiest of all option strategies because there is no limit on how high the stock's price could rise.

When you write a call, you receive a premium payment for it. As the writer, you are hoping the option is not exercised, which means it does not come "in the money." In this case, you have collected a payment and escaped any further commitment. When you make a covered call, consider the stock's price to be the market price minus the premium you receive, thus the stock's "basis" cost to you is reduced.

Writing a naked call is risky, as you are exposed to a loss not restricted in any way and that depends on how high the shares rise. When you take the position of writing a covered call, by already owning or buying the shares you are in a much more sound position. The best outcome with either the naked or the covered call is the price of the shares does not rise to the level of the strike price, and you keep the premium.

Only sell enough calls for the number of shares you own. In fact, there are times when you might not want to sell that many calls. Each call covers 100 shares, and every call you sell creates a potential obligation to sell 100 of your shares at the strike price, regardless of how high the market price has risen. This should not be thought of as a risk in the strategy, as it still represents a profit and perhaps a lost opportunity. A covered call has a limited upside, as the most you will receive for your shares is the strike price. Therefore, have a neutral to slightly bullish view of the shares. Shares that explode upwards in price would cause you to regret the lost opportunity, and shares that decline in price would not be a good holding in the first place.

Some novice option traders believe they should write covered calls against the stocks they believe will fall in value. When you sell a call, you receive a payment that gives the buyer the option to buy the stocks at a certain price. So, if the stocks fall in value, you collect the premium and have no risk of the option being exercised, but this point of view pays no attention to the overall picture, as the covered call writer owns or is long on the shares and a loss of value will impact his or her total portfolio. A call option is always worth less than the stock, so the stock is your most important asset and you do not want it to lose its value.

Given that there are a range of values and months associated with any option, you may be wondering how best to decide which call option to sell. There is no one correct or "best" answer because it depends on your objectives. The premiums vary depending on your selection of strike price and time to expiration.

First, select a strike price out of the money, at the money, or in the money. If you never want to lose the shares so you can continue selling more calls as each expires, consider writing calls out of the money, with higher strike prices. Ideally, you would hope the stock price rises to nearly the strike price because then you would gain from the premium and appreciation on the stock. The problem is the premiums will not be large. If you enjoy high returns with this method, it would probably be because of increasing stock value rather than from the premium collected.

Having said that, the classic covered call is probably an at-the-money front month option, the option choice that expires the soonest. The point of the covered call is to collect a good premium from an option expiring quickly, and the best means for that is an at-the-money strike. The larger premium means a lower cost basis on the stock, which gives a better downside hedge. There is no room for stock appreciation, but the higher premium compensates and makes an at-the-money option less risky.

Also consider writing in the money calls. This is a strategy with less risk and lower returns. Newcomers often wonder how you can profit by buying a stock at one price and giving someone else the right to buy it from you at a lower price, which on the surface sounds absurd. What it does not take into account is the way options are priced. All call options are worth at least their intrinsic value plus some time value, so if you sell an in-the-money call, you will be paid more than the value you are giving away. Obviously, you are much more likely to have the shares called away from you each time and be required to setup the complete covered call again.

With regard to the expiration date, you are usually much better off writing shorter terms because these are more expensive per unit of time and the value decays quickly, which is what you want as the writer. You could consider longer terms, on the basis you would receive a greater premium and this will provide bigger compensation against the stock price falling.

Writing covered calls is a safe strategy, and if, as you hope, the call expires worthless, you are free to write another covered call using the same shares and collect another premium. It is a way to derive a regular income from holding shares, regardless of whether they pay a dividend.

Naked Put

Not so well known as the covered call but with a similar risk-reward profile, selling naked puts is a conservative strategy despite the initial appearances and what your broker may tell you. Your broker may even require you to apply for a higher level of options investing if you want to trade naked puts. As opposed to "covered," naked refers to the fact you do not own any shares.

The naked put is a bullish investment. You will make a profit if the stock maintains its current price level or increases in value before the expiration of the option. However, unlike purchasing a long call option or buying the shares, with a naked put, your profits do not increase as the stock goes up in value. The profit is purely the premium the naked put seller receives.

The seller of a put option receives a premium and, in return, is obligated to buy shares of the underlying stock if required by the option buyer. In other words, the option buyer has bought the right to "put" or sell the shares to the option writer at the strike price, and if the strike price is above the current market price, the option will be exercised. The variables are the strike price and the time until the expiration date, which will affect the premium for the option.

The more conservative investors may consider using a naked put if they are interested in owning the shares but feel they are too highly priced. As an alternative to buying the shares outright, these investors will sell out-of-the-money options, which means the current price of the stock is higher than the strike price. While the stock remains over the strike price, the investor can continue to sell put options and replace them as each expires worthless and deriving a regular income. If the stock falls to the strike price or below, the option writer will be forced to buy the shares, but it will be at the target price they were willing to pay in the first place.

A more aggressive use of naked puts is to sell put options for a higher premium in order to get a higher return. This carries with it the risk the price will drop below the strike price, and the trader will have to take a loss. The option seller is in a better position than the trader who simply invests in the shares because of the premium received. This means the potential loss is less than faced by the stockholder.

If you intend to use naked puts, remember it is a bullish strategy and you want to identify stocks that hold the same price or increase in price. Ideally, you will write the put option, receive a premium, and the stock will increase in price so the option is not exercised. Despite this, there may be times when the unexpected happens and the stock is put to you. As long as you ensure the stock is one you would not mind owning for the long term, this is not such a bad outcome. Although you may have been incorrect about the stock's bullishness in the short term, if you are right in the long term, you have still made a good investment. Do not write puts on the stock unless you are bullish about it.

Spreads

An options strategy unrelated to "spread betting," spread in option terminology refers to buying one option and selling another at the same time. The options must be of the same type: call or put. If you are trading in futures contracts, you can also create a spread by buying one contract and selling another at the same time. In this case, you may buy the contract for one month and sell the contract for a later month, with the expectation the difference between the two contracts will move in your favor. Depending what differences you choose to have between the two options, there are many different results.

Vertical spreads

So called because the tables of option prices usually have the value down the left column and the months across the top, vertical spreads comprise two options in line vertically and usually adjacent, meaning the adjacent values of options expiring in the same month. Of all the combinations of options that can comprise a spread, the vertical spread is probably the easiest to understand. It offers limited risk and limited rewards.

First, let's suppose you could buy a $40 call and sell a $45 call in ZZZ Drilling, both with the same expiration date. This would be called a $40/$45 vertical spread and is also known as a bull call spread. It would be considered a long position because you had to spend a net amount of money to achieve it, as the $40 call is bound to be more valuable than the $45. It can also be called a "debit spread" for the obvious reason that it cost you money. Depending on the actual value of the shares when you do this, you will spend and receive different amounts for taking this position. As an example, suppose the $40 call cost $3 and you sold the $45 call for $1, which means your net outlay was $2 per share.

Now, if the stock does not go above $40, you will not exercise the $40 call, and the $45 call will not be exercised against you, so you lose the full $2 per share. However, if you take this type of vertical spread, called a bull spread, it is because you think the shares are going to increase in price. Let's assume they increased to $45 per share. In this case, you would exercise your $40 call and make $5 per share, which would give you a net profit of $3 per share. If the share price increased to more than $45, you would again exercise your $40 call, but the buyer of the $45 call would exercise against you and take those shares for $45 each, giving you the same $5 gain and $3 net profit. Therefore, your losses are limited to $2 per share, and your profits are limited to $3 per share. Your breakeven price would be $42 per share when you are able to exercise and call for the shares at $40 and sell them on for $42, which would cancel out your net option cost.

You can achieve the same effect by using two put option contracts. You could buy the $40 put option and sell the

$45 put option. In this case, the higher value option would be more expensive, so this would be a "credit spread" and you would receive money when you took out the position. If it was in line with the call option pricing, as it should be, you would receive $3 per share.

Examine what you have achieved. By selling the $45 put, you have the obligation to buy the shares at $45, which would be exercised if they are trading at any price up to that. However, you have the right to sell the shares for $40 if they are worth less at expiration. So the most you can lose is $5 per share, for a net loss of $2 after adding in the premium you received. If the shares are instead trading above $45, neither option will be exercised, and you keep the $3 net profit. The breakeven is again $42, and this vertical spread using put options has exactly the same effect as the previous one with call options.

Note that both of these bull spreads are created by buying low and selling high, whether it is call options or put options. In a similar way, it is possible to create vertical bear spreads, with which you are anticipating the price will fall. In this case, you sell low and buy high, again using either both call options or both put options.

Hedging With Options

Hedging in the financial world is a process of sacrificing the possibility of ultimate gain in order to protect your position. You must be willing to give up some upside potential in order to sustain less damage if things turn against you.

Most people try to avoid risk, but an even more powerful emotion is to avoid loss, and hedging is a powerful tool to reduce loss. It is in the nature of options to allow you to hedge.

Stock swap

This is probably the easiest hedging technique to understand, but for some reason is underutilized by most traders. It is useful when you have picked a stock with a good uptrend but are not sure how long it will continue to rise. Without options, you would have to take a guess. If you sold for a good profit, you might find the price continued to climb and you missed a major part of the move. On the other hand, if you kept the shares, you might find the price pulls back, and you did not realize the profit you could have had.

The answer to this is to sell the stocks for a profit and buy a call option for the same number of shares. By doing this, you have locked in most of the profit because the options will require a premium, but you still have the options to secure a profit from any further increase in price.

A hypothetical example will help explain the concept. Remember each stock option is for 100 shares. Suppose you were following the oil industry and decided the exploration group ZZZ Drilling was a good prospect, so you bought 1,000 shares at $20 each. This would cost you $20,000 minus a minimal commission if you were using a discount broker. Your instincts proved correct, and the shares rose to $40 each. Without options, you could now choose to sell the shares to make $20,000 in profit and wonder how much higher they might have gone, or you could hold onto the shares and hope there is not a retracement. Perhaps the wells they are drilling will turn out not to have the reserves expected, and the shares will crash back. You might also have considered selling a portion of the shares, which would mean taking some profit but diluting the future potential.

Instead, you can use a stock swap strategy. This requires selling all your shares and buying the equivalent amount of call options. Effectively, you are swapping your stock for options. You would sell 1,000 shares and buy 10 call options, which if they were at the money would cost you about $1.50 per share. Your shares would sell for $40,000 (1,000 multiplied by $40), and the options would cost you $1,500 (1,000 multiplied by $1.50), which gives you a net credit of $38,500. Instead of making 100 percent on your original investment, because you bought options, you made 92.5 percent — so far. However, you have locked in the profit, and you are still effectively long 1,000 shares because of your options.

The cost of this hedge is the price you pay for the options. For all share prices above $38.50 ($40 minus $1.50), you would make more by continuing to hold the shares. However, by making a stock swap into options, you have locked in the profit and minimized your downside while still having excellent upside potential.

Another point to note is you do not need to worry about timing the trade. It does not matter whether you are at the peak stock price or not because you have set yourself up to profit from any additional gains. Statistically, it is probably unlikely you are selling at the peak price, but that is of little consequence.

If the stock price continues to climb, you can lock in further gains by a process called "rolling up" the calls. Again, as it is a hedging technique, you will not lock in the full amount the stock has risen, but you will have secured additional profits against any downturn.

Suppose the price rose to $50 per share, and you wanted to lock in the additional profit. To roll up the calls, you would simultaneously sell your $40 call to close and buy the $50 call to open. This is a vertical spread, which would cost about seven dollars, so this is the credit you would receive in your account. These funds added to your account for the ten calls would be $7,000. Not as much as the shares have increased in price, but this additional amount is locked in, and you are still effectively long 1,000 shares for any additional profits. This demonstrates how powerful options can be.

Long stock with protective put

The long stock with protective put option strategy involves stock ownership or a long-stock position. The protective put trade gives, in essence, some downside insurance that limits your possible losses. It is a bullish strategy: you believe the market is going to go up, and it is conservative with an emphasis on limiting risk.

The profit from this trade comes from an increase in the stock price. The long protective put limits any loss in price because if the stock declines, you have the option to put or sell the shares at the strike price.

The cost of this insurance is the price of the option, so to break even, you are anticipating the stock value going up. Unlike the spreads, this combination trade allows you to benefit more as the stock price rises, so subject to the option cost deduction, you profit nearly as much as you would have done from just holding the stocks while limiting your risk.

Commonly, you would purchase the shares and buy a put with a strike price at the purchase price. Suppose you bought the shares for $40 each, and the put with a strike of $40 cost you $3, then you need the share price to beat $43 before you broke even, discounting commissions. Remembering each option covers 100 shares, you might buy 100 shares for $4,000 and pay $300 for the put option. The total outlay would be $4,300. If instead of rising in value, the shares dropped, it would not matter how far the price went down; you could still put them at $40 each, which means you would not have less than $4,000.

You can vary the amount of insurance you buy with this method by choosing a different strike price for the protective put. Never buy more time than you need. The protective put is similar to a long call position, and you can compare the costs for either method. This is a good choice to limit your downside risk, but the disadvantage is the protection is often somewhat expensive and would need to be renewed after expiration. This strategy makes sense if the volatility is low, when the put will be a more reasonable price. It can be used to protect gains when you have a long stock position you do not want to exit yet. This is another way of rolling up your gains without selling stocks.

Collar

The collar option strategy, sometimes called a fence, is a combination of three separate trades, a long stock, a long put, and a short call. It is really a combination of a covered call and a protective put, and it is conservative and bullish in outlook. Again, you are looking for an increase in the price of the stock to make a profit, but in this case, you have a limited downside and a limited upside, similar to the bull call spread.

The loss may be less than using a spread, depending on the option prices, and may even be zero or a guaranteed profit. Usually the collar trades that give the best risk/reward are at least a year in duration, and this does entail tying up your capital for a long time in the stock purchase. Be sure to check out the corresponding bull call spread, which may give a better result in a shorter time and tie up less cash.

Long put

Turning now to the bearish options, one of the simplest is the long put that stands to profit as the underlying falls in value. This should be considered an alternative to short selling stock, which has an unlimited downside if the stock increases in price, whereas the loss on the long put is limited to the cost of the option.

As with all option contracts, this put option may be sold for a higher price, and you do not have to wait for expiration in order to realize the profit. If the stock does start declining in value, it is likely the option can be sold for more than you paid, and then you need to consider whether to take the early profits or wait to see if the option becomes worth even more. The most profit for a put buyer is always the strike price minus the premium paid for the put, which would be achieved if the stock price fell to zero.

Neither a Bear nor a Bull

There are some interesting option combinations in which you may have a neutral stance on whether it is a bear or a bull market, but you still stand to profit from them.

Straddle

If you make a straddle trade, the only question you need to answer is whether you think the stock is going to make a big move or whether it is going to stay in a small range of prices. It does not matter if the price goes up or down, as the straddle is neutral to the direction of movement.

A straddle trade is made up of a put option and a call option in the same stock, at the same strike price, and with the same expiration date. All you must do is decide whether the stock is poised for a substantial move up or down or whether it will remain at the same price level. A long straddle is placed when the stock price is expected to increase in volatility and move away from its current level. It comprises buying the put and call option for the stock. The total amount of risk is the premium paid for these options.

The long straddle has unlimited potential profit to the upside and the downside until the stock price reaches zero. The worst case is if the stock continues to trade at its strike price, which gives a total loss of the premium. The breakeven is when the stock price moves either up or down by the total amount of the premium.

The alternative position, if you feel the price is not going to change much, is a short straddle trade, the opposite of the previous trade and consists of selling a put and a call on the same stock at the same strike price with the same execution date. In this case, you pay a premium, and this is the limit of your profits on the transaction. Your risk can be unlimited if the price changes. You only realize your maximum profit if the stock stays exactly on the strike price; otherwise, you will have to pay out on either the put or the call.

Strangle

A strangle is similar and can be used when you have no bias regarding the direction the stock price may take. The difference from a straddle is there are different strike values for the put and the call. By accepting a spread between the strike prices, the options will be cheaper to purchase, but you will have your maximum loss of the premium paid for a range of prices, from one strike price to the other. Otherwise, the strangle is similar to the straddle, and you make more profit the more the share price moves.

As with the straddle, it is possible to take a short position on a strangle trade, and your profit is limited to the premiums received, but you will realize this over a range of prices. Your loss can be unlimited if the share price is volatile.

Butterfly

As a further development from the straddle and strangle combination trades, you can also consider the set of butterfly trades. These are neutral in bias toward whether the share price will go up or down but seek to profit from predicting whether there will be little underlying stock movement or if there will be substantial price movement. A butterfly trade has four options at three different strike prices.

An explicit example will make this clearer. ZZZ Trading is trading at $40 per share. A long butterfly would buy one 35 call, sell two 40 calls, and buy one 45 call. There is likely to be a small net cost for this, which is the limitation of your risk. A long butterfly wins if the price does not change much. If the price ends at 40, you make five from your 35 call, and the other calls expire worthless. If the price ends at 35 or less, all the calls expire worthless, and you lose your net premium. If the price goes to 45 or more, your long calls pay for your out-of-pocket cost on the calls you sold, and again, you are just down by your net cost. Between 35 and 45, your profit varies.

There are several other ways options can be combined, sometimes with stock ownership, to create the risk/reward you want. Options allow you to limit your risk at the expense of some profit, which is basically the definition of hedging.

Long Futures

The advantage of using futures for speculation on a rising market is the leverage you can obtain. For a basic futures position, you can employ technical analysis in the same way as when you analyze stocks directly to determine when the price looks set to rise. It is popular to take a futures position in an index, such as the NASDAQ 100, as this builds in a degree of diversification that would be hard to emulate by buying individual stocks.

The NASDAQ 100 futures index trades at the CME. The value of the contract is $100 times this level, or around $180,000, but because of the leverage, the initial margin is only $17,500 with a maintenance margin of $14,000.

The futures price is usually a few points above the current value of the index, as there is typically some cost of carry built in. If you assume for the sake of the example the NASDAQ 100 climbs to 50 above the contract level, less than a 3-percent increase, this would net a profit of 50 times $100, or $5,000, a substantial profit based on your initial margin.

If $17,500 represents too large a percentage of your trading account to place in one trade, a series of smaller contracts called e-mini contracts are traded at the CME, and they are 1/5 the size of a regular contract. Of course, your profits would be reduced proportionately, but so would the margin requirements, and they may help you get started in futures trading. As always, it should be pointed out that futures are a leveraged product, and you can lose more than your initial deposit if your trade does not work out. It is best to keep the size of your trades down, particularly when you are beginning.

If there are one or two stocks in the index you do not like, you can create your own index by buying the regular index contract and shorting the contracts of the companies you do not like in the correct proportions, effectively creating a NASDAQ 98 index.

Short Futures

If you think the stock or index is about to fall, it is easy to sell a futures contract to open a short position. The initial margin requirement is similar, which is an advantage if you want to short a stock. If you were to take a short position directly in a stock, the margin requirement would be 50 percent of the value, so it is much more reasonable to trade a futures contract.

Another advantage of using a futures contract to short stocks is the manner in which stocks are usually shorted. Your broker needs to find shares that can be borrowed in order to sell them to establish your short position, and occasionally, the original owner may require the shares returned before you wish to close the position. Both of these circumstances can complicate the process. Against this, futures contracts have a built-in time limit you do not have when dealing directly with stocks, but it is easy to roll the contracts forward. If you have a short contract, when the expiration approaches, you can buy it back and sell another contract for a later month.

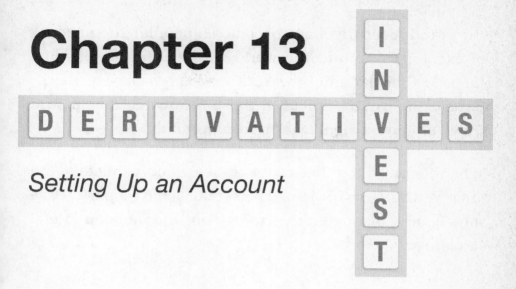

Chapter 13

Setting Up an Account

The Exchanges

As we saw in the history chapter, futures were originally developed to transfer the risk involved in the day-to-day business of buying and selling grain and agricultural products. These contracts are still traded in Chicago, but futures contracts have developed over the years to embrace many different products. In fact, wherever there is a degree of risk in pricing or delivery, there is potentially a futures market.

Most of the agricultural trading still takes place in Chicago at the Chicago Board of Trade (CBOT) and the Chicago Mercantile Exchange (CME). Foreign currency futures are also actively traded in Chicago at the International Monetary Market of the CME.

Stock index futures have become so popular the majority of exchanges around the world will deal in one or more indices. Chicago and New York exchanges played a large part in the establishment of these futures contracts, and they still have a significant trading volume.

When it comes to other commodities, such as metals and energy, the New York markets play a large part. Base metals are also actively traded on the London Metal Exchange (LME).

The Brokers

In recent years, picking a broker has become more difficult, with a greater choice. It used to be a good broker was one who had profitable ideas he or she would share with clients, but as the trading public has become more knowledgeable, there is less emphasis on this aspect. After all, no one cares about your money more than you do. The other potential conflict with this type of broker-client relationship is the broker obtains commissions or fees whenever trades are made, which some might say would tempt the broker to overtrade or "churn" your account.

Nowadays, you have a choice of using a discount broker who charges less commission but may not help with trading ideas if you are prepared to do your own research. A full service broker has the advantage of having a research department and will help you develop a strategy. With the amount of information online, many people are turning to a discount broker for their trading, and in this case, all that is necessary, in essence, is the broker fills orders efficiently and has a database of prices and information from which you can do your own research.

That said, ensure your broker is well capitalized and safe, and the larger discount brokers such as Scottrade and Etrade provide more stability and may possibly have better contacts on the trading floor to squeeze out better prices. To be able to implement futures trading, your broker must be licensed by the National Futures Association (NFA), which makes sure the licensees understand the legalities and technicalities of the exchange. They have a toll-free telephone number (1-800-621-3570) for you to check whether there have been any doubtful dealings associated with the brokerage, and they also have online resources ,found on their website at **www.nfa.futures.org,** where you can search by phone or individual name. Note that passing the licensing test for the NFA does not necessarily make them experts in analyzing and understanding the markets, so you must always be careful to do your own homework.

If you plan to do most of your trading online, make sure the brokerage has a solid, easy-to-understand Web presence. There may be times when you are unable to get through on the Web, so you also need a backup telephone number and contact in case you are holding open trades and need to close your positions.

Although commission rates are important, they can eat into your profits (similarly with spreads), so they should not be the sole arbiter of which broker you will sign up with. Do not spend a fortune in fees, and make sure any trading interface is easy to use. It can be helpful to interview the broker you will be dealing with most, at least on the telephone, to make sure he or she understands your requirements and experience. The telephone should be answered promptly, and the broker should be supportive if you need assistance with the type of order.

Opening an Account

Once you have selected your broker, the next step is to open an account. The paperwork is usually straightforward and requires standard information as well as a financial review. Expect your credit report to be accessed, as margin trading includes an element of risk for the broker who will want to check your creditworthiness.

It is the broker's obligation to have regard for your experience and look after your best interests. You will be required to sign off on disclaimers that acknowledge the risk of futures trading, and it is ultimately your responsibility whether you lose the money in your account or even more. However, the broker has a duty of care in making sure you are informed, qualified, and competent to take those decisions.

As with all types of trading, the money you set aside for the purpose should not be money you need for the basic costs of living or for paying your mortgage. Inevitably, such funds have too much emotion attached to them, and you will be unable to trade in a detached manner so you can follow your plan. The amount of money you deposit in the account has a direct bearing on your success, as a series of losses on a small account will serve to make it dysfunctional. Although you can begin with less, such as $5,000, you are much more likely to become a consistent trader if you have an account of $20,000 to start with. However much you have available, practice using a demo account before placing your money at risk. You must practice until you feel confident about what you are doing.

Futures Contracts

Depending on which commodities you intend to trade, there are different factors you must know about before committing your money. First, as mentioned in Chapter 3, the contracts are standardized, and though you may never take delivery, you must familiarize yourself with the conditions.

The unit size of contract is important, if only to know what you are getting into every time you place a trade. If you are speculating on grains, such as corn, each contract is for 5,000 bushels, and it is common practice to buy one contract by saying "Buy five corn," meaning five thousands of bushels. This is unique to the grain markets. As with every other futures contract, the number you ask for will be the number of contracts being traded.

Another important point with futures contracts is what is called a "tick value," the minimum amount by which the price fluctuates. This varies between commodities, so know how much one tick variation is worth for the contract. For instance, one tick for cattle represents $10 profit or loss.

When you come to select your trade, you will notice there are contracts for several different months available. Again, these are standard for the particular commodity you are looking at. The closest month to the current date is called the front, or spot, month, and the rest are called the back months. Usually, you will find the farther away the expiration date is, the more the contract will cost — effectively, this represents the increased cost of carry. Sometimes, there are exceptions, and the back months' contracts are cheaper than the spot month's contract. This can depend on which commodity or assets are being traded.

The best liquidity is usually in the front month, and this has the most activity. If you choose to trade in one of the back months, you may find it more difficult to get in or out of a position at the price you intend.

Placing Orders

Knowing the different types of orders to use can mean the difference between a profitable account and one that breaks even or even loses. Some markets are volatile, and unless you qualify your order, you can find you do not get the price you need.

If you place your order over the phone, note that many conversations are recorded for verification. If you make a mistake, you will be held liable for any losses, with the recording as evidence. If the broker makes a mistake, they will adjust your account accordingly. Either way, it is recommended you ask the broker or representative taking the order to repeat your order back to you, just to make sure it is clear and unambiguous.

If you are placing your order online, as many traders choose to do nowadays, double-check before confirming your instructions. The order may be automatically placed by a computer at the broker's office or it may be filled by personnel working there. Either way, expect a confirmation by e-mail or telephone call when it has been placed. Some types of orders may not be available online, so always know how to use the systems.

Market order

The simplest type of order you can give is a market order. To some extent, this is placing a great deal of trust in your broker because the order just commands your broker to buy or sell at whatever price he or she can. Depending on the market and the type of trading you are doing, the volatility in price works against you. Expect this type of order to be filled straight away, and in normal conditions, it will be within one or two ticks of the price you had hoped for, but there is no guarantee.

What is guaranteed is you will open the position you asked for. With some other types of orders, you may miss entering the market and lose out on a rapidly moving price. It is generally safer to issue other types of orders for your regular trading, as small slippages in the anticipated price may add up.

Limit order

Limit orders place a limit on the amount at which you will buy or sell the contract or assets, so when you place the order, you know what the cost will be. There are two types of limit orders. The buy limit order will only execute if the market reaches a specified price or better (less) for long enough for your broker to make the transaction. The sell limit order is similar, and the security will only be sold if the price goes up to or above the limit you put in for long enough.

The disadvantage to this is if the broker cannot complete the order at the price you specify, you will never open or close the position. The limit order gives you protection against buying at a higher price than you want to pay or selling too cheaply, and if these factors are important to your trading profits, there is no substitute.

Some brokers will charge more commission for placing anything other than a straight market order, so be clear before you start whether your broker has a differential pricing scale.

Stop orders

There are several different types of stop orders, and one of the more common uses is to protect you from incurring greater losses. The most basic use is when you have entered a long position, anticipating the market price will increase, and you place a stop loss order underneath the current price.

If your trade works out and the price increases, there is no effect from having the stop loss order in place. However, if the price falls until it reaches the level of the stop loss order, the order becomes a market order to sell. This has the effect of preventing you from losing too much on a failed trade, as it forces you out of the position.

As a note: You will not necessarily get the price you asked for in the stop loss order. Frequently, your order will be filled just slightly under that price, as the broker must sell immediately at the best price he or she can. In this case, the point is to mitigate your potential losses, and a market order in a declining market is the best way.

The stop loss order relieves you of the need to watch the market all day long in case of a downturn. When you place a trade and open the position, the next thing to do is settle on your stop loss level and put an order in place.

There are two potential disadvantages to the stop loss order. The first is some securities exhibit a lot of volatility, and the regular daily swings in price might hit your stop loss price and cause you to be closed out of the position at a loss when in fact the trade was fundamentally good and would have gone on to make you a profit. This points to the need to consider carefully how far below your entry level you are going to place your stop loss. This is an inherent part of your trading, as the amount of loss you risk should be limited to 2 percent of your account, and the stop loss level directly affects this.

The second potential disadvantage is if you place your stop loss order on the market, some traders believe major players will "stop loss hunt," manipulating prices to trigger your order to their advantage. Whether this is paranoiac or reality depends on the market you are in and how advantageous such behavior would be to the "hunter." Those who are concerned may wish to keep a note of the price level decided and watch the market so they can issue a sell order if the price falls.

Often prices tend to reach to and reverse at major whole numbers, such as $50, so a stop loss order at $49.95 is less likely to be falsely triggered than one at $50.05. If the calculated level is close to such a feature, you may wish to set it appropriately to avoid a nuisance stop out.

Another type of stop order is the trailing sell stop order, commonly called the trailing stop, which automatically adjusts the level at which the stop order is activated and the trade closed. The stop price automatically adjusts upward as the securities price increases. Usually, you can set a certain percentage or dollar amount for how far the stop level is below the price. When the price decreases, the stop level does not change. This means the increase in price is unlimited, but the trade is closed automatically once the price starts declining and hits the stop level.

These are the stop orders most frequently encountered and with which many traders are familiar. It is worth getting to know another use of stop orders, as sometimes it is also valuable. This is the buy stop order, and it is the opposite of the stop loss, or sell stop, order. The effect of this order is to buy the security if the price rises to the level set.

Although it can seem unusual to wait for the price to increase before buying, particularly as you may finish up paying even more than the level set — remember the order becomes a market order when the limit is reached — this can be a useful way to make sure you do not enter an order unless the situation looks promising. In particular, if the security is trading range bound and going sideways, you may be looking for a breakout from this pattern but are not sure if the price was going to remain restricted. In this case, a buy stop order at a level higher than the resistance might give you an answer. If the price remains range bound, the order does not trigger. If it does breakout, the order triggers as soon as this becomes apparent and will automatically open a position for you, whether you are watching the market at the time.

Buying and selling stock orders can also be used when your intention is to go short. In this case, the buy stop order would represent your stop loss position when in a trade, and the sell stop would open your short trade on a breakout.

Stop limit order

The stop limit order is also used in a similar way to the stop order and gives a better guarantee on price while not ensuring the order is filled. The stop limit order is a combination of the stop order and the limit order. First, the price must reach the stop price for the order to be attempted, and then it becomes a limit order that will be filled if the security is available at the limit price or better. Thus, the trade may not be executed, but you avoid the risk of execution at any price if the stock or contract price is volatile.

In the same way as the buy stop order mentioned above, you can anticipate an upward breakout in price by submitting a stop limit order just above the usual trading range. If the price does breakout, you will have opened a position as quickly as possible, subject to your limit price being available.

Order modifiers

Many of the orders given above can be combined with other instructions to ensure you get what you want. The market order, as it is executed immediately, does not take these modifiers.

First, for orders only executed under certain conditions, such as a limit order, you can control the timing. You have a choice of specifying a "day order," which means the broker will only watch the market and open your trade if the limit or other condition is met today. By tomorrow, if not executed, the order will be forgotten. If the order is placed after trading hours, it will be applied to the next day only.

Another common modifier is the "good till cancelled," or GTC, order. This one requires the broker to keep trying to place your order, at the conditions you specify, until you delete the order. Note that many brokers will allow GTC orders to lapse if the conditions are not met and the order activated within a couple of months, and usually, they will issue you a warning to this effect. Another similar modifier is the "good till date," and in this case, the broker will try to place the order in accordance with the conditions until the specified date, after which the order is void.

Finally, you can specify with a limit order that it is only executed if all the shares can be purchased in one lot at the required price. This is called an "all or nothing" (AON) condition.

Less common orders

The previous orders are generally applicable to most markets and are used often. Here are some others that are less well known and less widely applicable or available, but you may come across them and occasionally find them useful.

Market on close (MOC)

This is a specialized order directed at the broker on the trading floor. It instructs him or her to buy or sell for you in the last minute of trading. This may be regarded as urgent or desperate. It has the disadvantage of the market order in that you have no control over the price obtained and the extra danger in that the last minute of trading may give distorted prices. Generally, even if available, you will not want to use this type of order in your regular trading.

Buy or sell stop close only (SCO)

These are again orders executed in the last minute of trading and are not accepted at CBOT. The buy stop order will be executed if the market is at or above your order price, and your order will be filled as whatever price the floor broker can get. The sell stop close only order is the opposite, and with the market price at or below the order price, again the order will be filled at whatever price is available on the floor.

Market not held

Sometimes known as the disregard tape order (DRT), this order is similar to a market order, but it instructs the floor broker to use his or her best judgment in filling the order and not to be constrained by any time limit. Obviously, with this order, you put a lot of trust in the broker and cannot hold him or her liable if they give you a bad fill.

This type of order could be useful if you are dealing in a large number of shares or securities, as it allows the broker to exercise more skill rather than taking whatever they can in order to complete your order expeditiously.

Fill or kill (FOK)

This order is entered with a specific price and instructs your broker to either execute it at that price immediately or cancel (kill) the order. In practice, the floor broker will try to execute the order three times in succession before killing it.

This type of order gives you immediate feedback from the market, so you do not have to wait to find out whether your order has been filled. The specific prices should not be far away from the current market price so the broker has a chance of succeeding in filling the order. If you enter several FOK orders that cannot be filled, you run the chance of annoying your broker who has to spend time and effort in trying to satisfy them.

Contingent orders

These are orders in which individual execution depends on other factors, such as another order being canceled.

One cancels the other (OCO)

As you might expect, this consists of two orders, the second one of which is a contingency should the first one not take place. Perhaps you are day trading and want to close your position at the end of the day regardless of the price. At the same time, once you enter the trade you want to put in place a stop loss order in case it does not go your way.

The answer to this would be to place a sell stop loss order OCO MOC. This means that if your stop loss is hit, the MOC order is canceled, but if the trade goes your way and your stop loss does not need to take place, you exit your position at the end of the day with the market on close (MOC) order, which would in turn automatically cancel your stop loss order.

Cancel replace

When you have a pending order and you want to amend it, it is usually easy to edit it online. If you are giving verbal direction, to be sure you instruct your broker you have a cancel replace order, state the order you are canceling and give the new order.

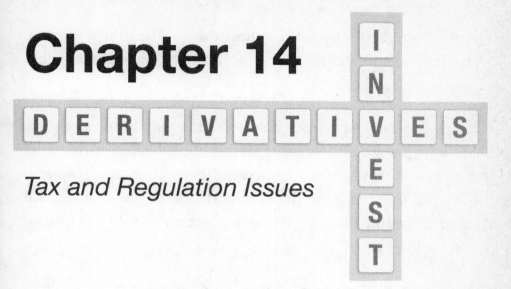

Chapter 14

DERIVATIVES

Tax and Regulation Issues

There are some interesting differences in tax treatment between different countries. For example, unlike the United States, in Great Britain, the proceeds of betting wins are not taxed, and this has resulted in spread betting gaining favor in the markets. There is also no capital gains tax charged, and provided the investor has another form of income, spread betting does not attract income tax either.

In the United Kingdom, an investor buying shares has to pay stamp duty to the government. As derivatives allow investors to profit as if they owned the shares without taking actual ownership, equity futures and contracts for difference (CFD) do not require stamp duty to be paid and have, therefore, become popular.

Arguably, the United States will be missing a potential revenue source if the rules are not changed in the coming years to permit the U.S. trading community to use CFDs.

Even though the tax and stamp duty issues do not arise, the leverage available and the flexibility have made them popular elsewhere.

Equity swaps can also result in tax advantages. If, for instance, a foreign investor were considering purchasing shares but would be restricted in his or her ownership and required to pay tax on the dividends, he or she can instead setup a swap with a dealer who is not subject to tax or who can reclaim it.

The swap dealer would borrow money to buy the shares and, through the swap contract, pay the total return on the shares, including gross dividends, to the investor. In return, the investor would make regular payments to the dealer that would cover the interest on the loan and a profit or charge for the dealer's services.

Regulation

The differences in regulation between countries are also worth noting. Contracts for difference are a fairly recent invention that has caught on in England and Australia in particular. They get around the stamp duty requirement and give a leveraged product that enhances stock-picking rewards. In the United States, CFDs are not permitted by the SEC, the chief regulating body for financial matters.

In the United States, futures trading is regulated by the Commodity Futures Trading Commission (CFTC), established in 1975 by Congress. This requires everyone involved with serving the public and executing orders to be registered. There are different classifications for registering, depending on what function the person is performing, and registration is taken care of by the National Futures Association (NFA) for the Commission. The types of registration include the following:

Futures commission merchant (FCM)

An FCM is an individual or company that takes orders to buy and sell futures contracts or options on futures and receives money for the orders.

Introducing broker (IB)

The IB solicits and may accept orders but does not directly handle the money or assets to buy or sell the contracts.

Commodity pool operator (CPO)

If an individual or business solicits funds for or operates a commodity pool, they must be registered as a CPO. This includes people who group together to invest in futures or options on futures, unless 15 or fewer people handle less than $400,000.

There are some other exemptions to this registration, including whether the business is already regulated, such as a bank or a registered investment company.

Commodity trading advisor (CTA)

The commodity trading advisor is authorized to advise others on the value of futures and commodity contracts and on buying and selling particular contracts. He or she receives compensation for it. This advice may be either directly or indirectly given, so for example, a newsletter may be considered exercising trading authority over the individual's account.

There is an exception for newsletters and periodicals if the advice is general and not based on knowledge of the customers' circumstances.

Associated person (AP)

An AP can solicit orders on behalf of one of the foregoing registrants and is a salesperson or sales manager for them.

Principal

The principal is defined by financial ownership and being in charge of a company. No registration is required, but principals must file the appropriate forms.

Floor broker (FB)

A floor broker has trading privileges and will purchase or sell futures contracts or options for another person.

Floor trader (FT)

The floor broker has floor trader privileges without further registration. The floor trader can buy or sell futures contracts or options on futures for his or her own account.

The idea behind these registrations is the public is protected from unfair trading practices, financial risks, and dishonest sales practices. The performance of people in the industry is monitored, disclosures are required, and a minimum amount of capital for firms doing business is specified.

12/

Key investment
ratios and measures

Conclusion

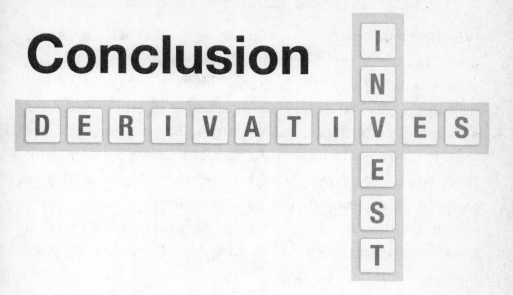

In this book, we have discussed derivatives of all shapes and sizes, and it should be clear derivatives are not intrinsically evil and can perform useful hedging functions. The fact they have been blamed, rightly, for the severity of the financial crisis in recent years is a consequence of their imprudent usage by people concerned with extracting the last drop of profit from their trading and is not an inherent fault with the system that offers derivatives.

However, beyond the hedging function, derivatives do offer speculators the opportunity to use their skill and expertise to multiply the effectiveness of their investments. If you are tempted toward such speculation, this in itself is an understandable attitude, but make sure you are fully aware of the risks as well as the rewards. This book should have opened your eyes to the pitfalls as well as the opportunities.

Whichever derivatives you choose to trade, there are some basic elements you need to address so you approach the prospect in a way that is more likely to succeed. First, Chapter 11 talked about constructing a plan, essential for successful trading of all sorts. It may be possible by sheer luck to start trading derivatives and make a fortune, and there are tales of people who have done this; sometimes those tales also include the postscript that the same people lost a fortune in the next year of trading. To make a consistent gain, be prepared to follow through with your plan.

Trade with money you are prepared to lose and do not be overly optimistic. Be brutal in cutting your losses if your plan does not work out as you expected, and review your plan at regular intervals. If it is not working well for you, determine how you can improve it.

The first thing to do after entering a trade, no matter how promising it may look, is to set your stop loss at the place you know it should go. When you decided to make the trade, one of your actions will have been to look at the potential risk against the possible reward to be sure the odds were in your favor. Therefore, you already know the downside risk and where to exit the trade. With a predetermined stop loss level, you will be prepared for rapid turnarounds and not be tempted to let the trade run the wrong way on the basis it should come back at any moment.

If you are trading derivatives for speculative gains rather than using them in combination to hedge other trades, guard against using too much leverage. Using leverage of 30 to 1 was regarded as risky when U.S. banks did it, but you can easily fall into the same trap and find you have overextended your resources, so an inopportune move of the market will leave you without an answer. Just because you can leverage your capital to the hilt does not mean you should, and you must always be aware of the downside when considering the reserves you are using.

Finally, it is human nature to be affected by fear, greed, and your own ego. Stick with your plan, and modify it when necessary. Take your profits when due — and not before — but cut your losses as soon as it is apparent the trade has not worked. Never allow your ego to stand in the way of exiting a losing position by thinking you have it right despite the actions of the market. The market has more money than you and does not really care what you think it should do.

Take care, have fun, and make your money work for you.

Glossary

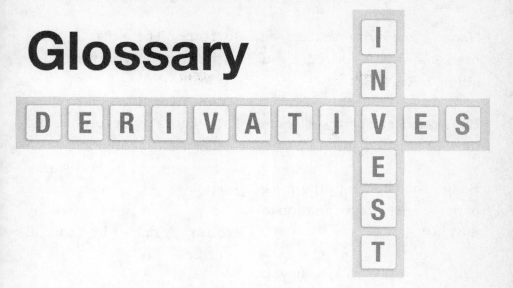

American option: A type of option that can be exercised on any date up to the expiration date.

AMEX: The American Stock Exchange.

Arbitrage: A system of taking profits risk-free by identifying a mispricing in the market.

Ask: The price for which you can buy a financial security at the brokers.

Assignment: The notification to the writer of an option that he or she must deliver the underlying at the exercise price.

At the money: When the strike price of an option is equal to the market price of the underlying, which gives an intrinsic value of zero.

Bar chart: A chart showing the price of a security against time. Price is on the vertical axis, and time along the horizontal. Each period, often one day, is represented by a vertical bar from the lowest to the highest price seen on that day.

Bear: One who thinks the market is overpriced and falling in value.

Bear market: A market where most prices are falling.

Beta: The change in the price of the security for a variation in the market.

Bid: The price at which you can sell a security.

Bid/offer spread: Difference between the bid price and the ask, or offer, price for a derivatives contract.

Binary option: An all or nothing financial instrument; effectively a form of betting whether a price will go up or down.

Black-Scholes model: An option pricing method developed in the 1970s.

Bond: A loan at fixed interest to a company or the government.

Bottom: The lowest price reached during a downtrend.

Breakout: A price movement that goes beyond the established fluctuations, such as the support or resistance levels.

Broker: A dealer in financial securities.

Bull: One who supports and expects an increase in prices on the markets.

Bull market: A market where the predominant trend is increasing prices.

Buying to cover: A tactic used when you have sold a call option. It entails buying shares to be ready if the option is exercised.

Call: A type of option, the buyer of which has the right to buy a stock at a certain price by, or sometimes before, the option expiration date.

Call away: What a broker may occasionally do when a trader has a short position. If the shares are needed by the original owner and cannot be replaced, the broker will immediately purchase the shares to replace them.

Candlestick chart: A chart showing the price of a security against time, similar to the bar chart and showing the same information but in a more graphical manner.

Cash settlement: The contract is settled in cash rather than through delivery of the underlying.

Chicago Board of Trade (CBOT): Opened as a commodity market and now includes futures and options contracts.

Chicago Board Options Exchange (CBOE): A major options exchange founded in 1973.

Chicago Mercantile Exchange (CME): A Chicago futures and options exchange.

Clearinghouse: An agency connected with the commodity exchange used for settling all futures contracts, whether by delivery or through financial settlement.

Commission: The fee charged by a broker for a service.

Commodity: Something physical traded on the market, such as cereals, oil and gas, meat, etc.

Contract for difference (CFD): A margined product where a trader may profit from moves in the underlying price without owning or paying for the underlying.

Cost of carry: The cost of holding a position in an asset; for example, interest and storage charges.

Covered call: A strategy in options trading that involves buying the shares for which you are selling a call option.

Credit default swap: A contract that provides a form of insurance against specific events, such as a borrower defaulting on a loan.

Cross currency swap: An interest rate swap where the payments are made in two different currencies.

Currency option: The right but not the obligation to exchange currencies at a predefined rate.

Day trader: A trader who concentrates on market moves during the day for his or her trades and usually does not hold any position overnight.

Delivery month: When a futures contract expires and delivery becomes due.

Delta: The change in the value of an option for a change in the value of the underlying.

Demand: Quantifies the amount of commodity that potential buyers would want to purchase at different prices and is inversely related to price. As the price goes up, demand goes down.

Derivative: A financial instrument that derives its value from something else, called the underlying.

Direct access broker: For the trader who wants direct access to the market, in order to see all the activity, the direct access broker can arrange the software and data feed required.

Discount broker: A broker who provides a share buying and selling service at a cheap price but does not necessarily give the service of a full-service broker.

Discount rate: The rate used to discount future cash flows to the present value for financial calculations.

Discretionary trading: Describes accounts at a brokerage where the customer has permitted the firm to execute trades without specific authorization for each one.

Dividend: A payment made at regular intervals by some companies to shareholders.

Dow Jones Industrial Average (DJIA): An index based on 30 U.S. industrial companies.

Downtrend: A period of time during which the price of a financial security is steadily falling on average.

ETF: An acronym for exchange-traded fund; often a collection of shares or securities in a particular sector or marketplace.

Elasticity of demand or supply: Relates the percentage of change in quantities demanded (or supplied) for a given percentage change in the price.

If demand is steady as price varies, it is inelastic. If price makes a big difference to the demand, it is elastic.

Elliott wave: A well-known theory relating to cyclical movements of prices; states they move in a series of waves.

Equities: Another name for stocks and shares.

European option: A type of option that can only be exercised at expiry. See also American option.

Exchange: A market where financial securities are traded.

Exercise: In the financial sense, to exercise an option is to take up the option because it is in profit.

Exercise price: The contracted price in the option contract.

Expiration date: The date when a futures or options contract must be fulfilled.

Exponential moving average: A method of calculating a moving average line, which places greater emphasis on more recent values.

Face value: The notional value of a debt security such as a bond.

Fair value: A theoretical value of a financial asset, often calculated using a pricing model.

Fibonacci ratios: Seek to define the ratios between different price levels to predict the market movements

Fill: The price at which your order is completed.

Fill or kill: A type of order that requires the broker to execute it totally at the specified price or cancel it.

Floating-rate: A rate of interest that varies over time, such as the LIBOR.

Foreign currency future: A contract requiring a later purchase or sale of a specified amount of money issued by another country.

Forex: Short for foreign exchange, the marketplace where currency transactions take place.

Forward contract: An agreement between two parties to buy and sell certain goods or securities at a fixed price on a future date.

Forward exchange rate: An agreed rate to exchange two currencies in the future.

Forward rate agreement (FRA): A contract to pay compensation based on the difference between a contracted interest rate and the actual market rate in the future.

Free riding: Selling a stock before it has been paid for during the three-day settlement period.

FTSE 100 index: A market index for the top 100 UK shares, weighted by market capitalization.

Full-service broker: Sometimes known as the traditional stockbroker, this dealer will offer advice and assistance in your trading.

Fundamental analysis: Concerned with valuing a company from its basic or fundamental factors, such as the value of buildings and equipment, the amount of sales, the profit on each sale, expenditures, etc.

Futures contract: A commitment to buy or sell a commodity or security for an agreed price at a certain date in the future.

Futures option: An option to buy or sell a futures contract.

FX option: An option to exchange two currencies at a fixed rate.

Good till canceled order (GTC): An order to your broker to buy or sell at a fixed price. The order remains open until fulfilled at that price or canceled by you.

Government securities: Bonds, notes, and bills issued by governments.

Greeks: A series of factors that define option sensitivities.

Head and shoulders: A charting pattern that often signals a reversal to a trend.

Hedge fund: A fund that takes long and short positions in securities with the intention of hedging investment against market losses. Can also take highly leveraged positions.

Hedging: A maneuver to guard against market losses.

Implied volatility: The volatility implied by an actual option price.

In the money option: An option that has a positive intrinsic value.

Index: A figure that represents the changing value of a basket of stocks in a particular market.

Index fund: A fund that invests to attempt to track the changes in an index.

Index option: An option on the future value of an index, such as the S&P 500.

Indicator: Used in technical analysis to help decide on the future price movement.

Initial margin: The amount required is a good-faith deposit to establish a new position in the futures or options markets.

Interest rate swap: An agreement between two parties to exchange future interest payments for a specified period. Usually, one rate is fixed and the other is based on a floating rate such as the LIBOR.

Intraday: Refers to price movements during the day, exploited by day traders.

Intrinsic value: The built-in value of an option disregarding time value. For a call option, it is the price of the underlying less the strike price.

Investor: A person who buys a financial security with the intention of owning it for a long time in the belief it will increase in value.

Level II: Describes a trading screen available to the public, which shows the bid and ask prices currently being offered by traders.

Leverage: A way of increasing the effectiveness of your trading capital, in practical terms, by using it as a deposit on a much larger trade.

LIBOR: Acronym for London InterBank Offered Rate, the official rates for bank lending in London.

Limit order: An order to your broker to buy or sell shares but with a limit to the price you are prepared to go to.

Line chart: A chart of stock or other financial security prices, drawn with a single line connecting the closing prices for each day.

Liquidity: A measure of the trading activity in a security, such that good liquidity means trading is easy and there are many buyers and sellers.

Long: The term used for buying and owning a share or security.

Maintenance margin: A system used in some markets, in which a margin call is issued if the account falls below a certain level.

Managed accounts: Accounts in which all trades are determined by the trading advisor or fund manager.

Margin: Refers to a facility to borrow money from your broker; buying on margin means you buy a security without paying in full.

Margin call: What a broker will do if a trade moves against the trader and he or she fails to meet the minimum funding requirements. The broker will call for more money to be deposited in the trader's account.

Mark-to-market: A system of revaluing investments while they are held based on the current market price.

Market order: A direct order to a broker to buy or sell at the best price he or she can at that time.

Moving average: A line plotted on a price chart that connects average price points for the previous X number of days.

MACD: Acronym for moving average convergence/

divergence, a chart indicator based on moving average computations.

Naked option: An option position not covered or hedged.

NASDAQ: Used to be an acronym but is now the proper name for one of the U.S. stock markets, mainly known for trading in technology companies.

Net present value (NPV): Used particularly for funds and is the sum of the present values.

NYSE: Acronym for New York Stock Exchange, one of the leading stock markets in the world.

Offer price: Also called the ask price and is the price at which the asset or contract is for sale.

One cancels the other order (OCO): An order that designates both sides of the trading range, or the same side with different months or prices, and when the condition of one order is reached the other is canceled.

Open interest: A measure of the number of futures contracts (or options) in existence. This is not the same as the volume, or amount traded, as it measures the total contracts not fulfilled.

Open position: Can be either a long or a short position in financial assets or contracts, which exposes the holder to market risk until the position is closed.

Option: Gives the buyer the right but not the obligation to buy or sell the underlying goods or security at a predetermined price by a set date.

Option holder: The person who buys the option.

Option writer: The person who accepts the premium for the option and is required to fulfill the option contract if needed.

Order: an instruction to your broker to deal in shares on your behalf.

Ordinary share: A stake in a public company that gives a right to take part in the running of the company, usually by voting at an annual meeting.

Oscillator: An indicator that moves between the extremes of overbought and oversold that indicates the current market sentiment.

Out of the money option: An option that has no intrinsic value; for example, when the strike price is above the underlying price for a call option.

Over-the-counter (OTC): Refers to dealing or trading directly rather than through an exchange.

Overbought: A signal given by a trading indicator, which suggests buying activity has gone on too long, and the share or security may be due to fall in value.

Oversold: The opposite of overbought. Usually signaled by a trading indicator, it suggests the security has been sold off to a lower level than its real value, and the price may recover in future.

Par: The face value or notional value of a bond, normally paid out at maturity.

Pattern day trading: When someone works at day trading and make a minimum number of trades, this person is considered a pattern day trader, which has consequences for his or her account size and tax position.

Physical delivery: The process of delivering the underlying commodity or asset specified in a derivatives contract.

Position trading: A longer-term form of trading with more emphasis on fundamentals and looking for trends continuing for some weeks.

Premium: The amount paid to buy an option contract.

Present value: The current discounted value of a future cash flow.

Price/earnings ratio (P/E): One of the fundamental factors about a company, the price versus earnings ratio is the ratio between the stock's current price and last year's earnings.

Protective put: Buying a put option to protect against losses on an asset.

Put: A type of option that gives it the right to sell a share at a predetermined price by a set date.

Pyramiding: Adding contracts to an existing profitable position.

Relative strength indicator (RSI): A momentum-based indicator used in technical analysis.

Resistance: Refers to a price level for a stock or security that the price goes up to but does not exceed, at least for the current trading pattern, i.e. there is a resistance to going higher.

Retracement: In an up or a downtrend, this is a temporary reversal in the trend.

Reversal pattern: A chart pattern that indicates the current trend of the stock price is likely to reverse.

Rho: The change in value of an option for any given change in interest rate.

Risk/reward: A calculation that should be done before every trade to determine if the possible gains are better than the possible loss.

Scalping: A method of trading that attempts to make many small gains quickly.

Securitization: The process of creating asset-backed securities, usually bonds backed by underlying assets.

Security: A general name for a financial instrument such as a share or bond.

Settlement date: The date when an asset is transferred and payment must be made.

Shares: Represent ownership in a company and are bought and sold on the stock markets.

Short: The opposite of long, to be short in a stock means to have sold shares you did not own with the hope that the price will go down and you can replace the shares more cheaply.

Short-term trading: The buying and selling of shares or other financial securities within a period of days or weeks with the intention of making a profit.

Simple moving average (SMA): Refers to a moving average line where the values are calculated by adding together the values for the previous X number of days and dividing by X.

Spot price or rate: The current market price or rate.

Spread: Used in some financial securities and in forex trading and is the difference between the price you can buy at and the price you are offered if you are selling. It is one of the ways a broker can make a profit.

Stochastic oscillator: A momentum-based indicator based on detailed price data.

Stocks: See shares.

Stock index: A number related to the value of a group of shares selected as representative of the market.

Changes in the index indicate the condition of the market.

Stock index future: A futures contract related to the value of the stock index.

Stock market: Traditionally a physical place where brokers and market makers meet each day to trade shares on the instructions of their clients. Increasingly, the place has become superseded by an electronic virtual market.

Stock option: An option to buy or sell a share at a predetermined price.

Stop loss: The name for an order that directs a broker to sell for a loss if a trade goes the wrong way; the stop loss order exits the trade before you incur further losses.

Straddle: A strategy used with options, either buying a call and a put for the same underlying with identical strike price and expiration or selling a call and a put for the underlying.

Strike price: The agreed price in an option contract.

Supply: The amount of a commodity or assets sold at a given price. Generally positively related to the price; an increasing price would encourage an increasing supply.

Support: A price level that a stock is not expected to go below based on previous charting history. See also resistance.

Swing trading: Trading in financial securities with holding periods of days, endeavoring to make a profit more quickly than an investor.

Technical analysis: The study of price, volume, and open interest of financial securities, through which future price movements are anticipated.

Time value: A measure of how much of an option or future price is attributable to the expiration date, as compared to the intrinsic value of the underlying.

Trading plan: Usually a written plan prepared by the trader, which summarizes how he or she intends to trade.

Trading range: The range of prices over which recent market action has been observed. Generally applies to a sideways market.

Trailing stop: A type of stop loss order where the order price changes, following the share price but never reducing.

Treasury bond, note, bill: Bond securities issued and backed by the government. The different names refer to different times until maturity.

Trend: Describes a steady and consistent price movement, either upward, downward, or even sideways, staying around the same price.

Underlying: The asset or commodity on which a derivative contract, such as a futures contract, is based.

Volatility: A measure of the fluctuations in price of a financial security.

Volume: Describes the amount of trading that takes place in a period.

Whipsaw: Used to describe what happens in a volatile market, in which price fluctuations are significant enough to cause traders to be stopped out of their trades by their stop loss orders, even though the overall trend was in their favor.

Writer: The person selling an option.

Yield: The return on an investment.

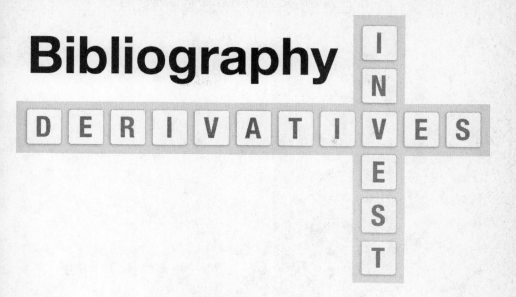

Bibliography

Bernstein, Jake, "How the Futures Markets Work", *New York Institute of Finance*, 2000

Chisholm, Andrew M., "Derivatives Demystified", *John Wiley & Sons*, 2004

Duarte, Joe, "Futures and Options for Dummies", *Wiley Publishing*, 2006

Durbin, Michael, "All about Derivatives – The Easy Way to Get Started", *McGraw-Hill*, 2006

Johnson, Bill, "The Single-Stock Futures Revolution", *21st Century Investor Publishing, Inc.*, 2002

Kaeppel, Jay, "The Four Biggest Mistakes in Futures Trading", *Marketplace Books*, 2000

McPhee, Stuart, "Trading in a Nutshell", *Wrightbooks*, 2008

Biography

DERIVATIVES INVEST

Alan Northcott is a successful financial author, freelance writer, trader, professional engineer, radio broadcaster, farmer, karaoke jockey, and wedding officiant, along with other pursuits. He and his wife live in Colorado where they share their house with many dogs and cats. They have three children living on three different continents and two grandchildren, one of whom, thankfully, also lives in Colorado, which means they get to see him grow up.

Originating from England, Northcott was educated at Eltham College in London and obtained his degree from the University of Surrey, also in England. He immigrated with his wife to America in 1992. His engineering career spanned more than 30 years on both sides of the Atlantic, and recent years have found him seeking and living a more diverse, fulfilling lifestyle. This is the seventh financial book he has written, all which are available from Atlantic Publishing Group, Inc.

He offers a free newsletter on various related and unrelated topics. Find out more at **www.alannorthcott.com**, or e-mail him directly at alannorthcott@msn.com.

Index

I
N
D E R I V A T I V E S
E
S
T

A

Arbitrage, 53-54, 112, 136-138, 265

Ask, 32, 56, 83-84, 88, 91, 101, 140, 158, 164, 188, 243, 245, 265-266, 272, 274

B

Bar chart, 185-186, 265, 267

Beta, 266

Bear market, 64, 181, 232, 266

Binary option, 266

Bond, 42, 44, 63-68, 127-128, 266, 270, 275, 277, 279

Bottom, 63, 182, 266

Breakout, 191, 249-250, 266

Broker, 56, 59, 82-87, 91, 105-106, 139-140, 150, 157-159, 194, 222, 227, 237, 240-242, 245-247, 251-254, 257-258, 266-268, 270-271, 273, 275, 277-278

Bull market, 64, 180, 183, 232, 266

C

Call away, 267

Candlestick chart, 186, 267

Cash settlement, 52, 58, 84, 267

Chicago Board of Trade, 41, 45-46, 267, 239

Chicago Board Options Exchange, 44-45, 267

Chicago Mercantile Exchange, 63, 239, 267

Clearinghouse, 59, 159, 267

Commodity, 24-29, 31, 42-43, 57, 60-62, 84-85, 102, 116, 118-119, 121, 135-136, 193, 197, 244, 256-257, 267-268, 271, 275, 278-279

Cost of carry, 56, 134, 136, 145-146, 150, 236, 244, 267

Covered call, 218-222, 231, 267

Credit default swap, 17, 110, 112, 268

Cross currency swap, 268

Currency option, 102-103, 268

D

Delta, 132, 152-153, 268

Day trader, 268, 275

Direct access broker, 268

Discount broker, 227, 240-241, 268

Discretionary trading, 269

Dividend, 86, 135, 140, 215, 217, 222, 269

Dow Jones Industrial Average, 90, 180, 269

Downtrend, 182-183, 195, 208-209, 266, 269, 276

E

Elliott wave, 181-182, 269

Equities, 196, 199, 64-65, 79, 89, 134, 269

Exercise, 31, 34, 96, 99, 110, 130, 142, 145, 150, 189, 215-218, 225, 252-253, 265, 269

Exercise price, 145, 265, 269

Exponential moving average, 192, 270

F

Fibonacci ratios, 270

Fair value, 136-138, 140, 270

Floating-rate, 155, 270

Foreign currency future, 75, 270

Fill or kill, 253, 270

Forex, 55, 83, 91, 100, 128-129, 137, 178-179, 188, 199, 270, 277

Forward exchange rate, 270

FTSE 100 index, 271

Full-service broker, 268, 271

Futures contract, 28-31, 34, 39, 42, 53, 57-58, 60, 67-73, 85, 94-95, 102, 130, 133, 138-139, 168, 174, 236-237, 243, 268-269, 271, 278-279

Fundamental analysis, 173-174, 190, 125-126, 271

Futures option, 44, 94, 103, 130, 271

G

Greeks, 39, 45-47, 151-152, 154, 271

H

Hedging, 53, 65, 70, 73, 103, 112, 139, 164-167, 169, 196, 226-227, 229, 235, 261, 271

I

Implied volatility, 149-151, 271

Indicator, 126, 132, 192, 194-196, 208, 272, 274-277

Initial margin, 71, 158-159, 235-236, 272

Interest rate swap, 36, 44-45, 108, 113, 157, 162, 268, 272

Intraday, 272

Intrinsic value, 142, 216-217, 221, 265, 272, 275, 279

L

Leverage, 31, 64-65, 74, 77, 80, 86, 91, 128-129, 131, 139, 158, 163-164, 167, 170, 188, 201-203, 213, 235, 256, 263, 272

LIBOR, 35-36, 57, 69-70, 108, 135, 270, 272

Limit order, 246, 250-252, 273

Liquidity, 24, 29, 41, 62, 65, 83, 131, 139, 182, 244, 273

M

MACD, 195, 273

N

NYSE, 41, 274

O

Open position, 158, 236, 245-247, 249, 274

Oscillator, 195, 208, 275, 277

Ordinary share, 275

Overbought, 194-195, 275

Oversold, 194-195, 275

P

Par, 275

Pattern day trading, 275

Premium, 34-35, 48, 97-98, 101-104, 110, 131, 133, 136, 141-142, 144, 150-152, 154-155, 168, 197, 218-223, 226-227, 232-235, 274, 276

Present value, 156-157, 268, 274, 276

Protective put, 168, 229-231, 276

Pyramiding, 276

R

Resistance, 189-194, 196, 209, 249, 266, 276, 278

Retracement, 122, 200, 228, 276

Rho, 152, 154-155, 276

S

Scalping, 80, 277

Spot price or rate, 277

Stochastic oscillator, 195, 277

Stop loss, 80-81, 200, 205-206, 209-210, 247-249, 253-254, 262, 278-279

Straddle, 232-234, 278

Strike price, 97-98, 110, 145-146, 151-152, 155, 168, 215-220, 222-223, 230, 232-234, 265, 272, 275, 278

T

Trailing stop, 210, 248, 279

Trading range, 191, 209, 249-250, 274, 279

V

Volatility, 45, 61, 79-81, 88, 116, 131-132, 145-151, 154, 201-203, 210, 231, 233, 245, 247, 271, 279

W

Whipsaw, 279